Valuing our Indigenous stories as we do allows us to be open to those from other cultures. By reading each other, we grow our ability to understand, to acknowledge and to share one another's joy, hope, grief, loss, and for many, the predicament of losing homes, lands, community, family and country. We are all people of stories.

Our stories define who we are and what we want to become, just as it was the stories of our ancestors that formed the basis of Aboriginal law, spiritual beliefs and an understanding of how to maintain a relationship with the land.

It is a basic need for all humans to be offered hands in friendship, to be offered shelter and to live in peace with a sense of security. This is how we can welcome and acknowledge all stories, and give them hearth in our hearts. It would not be within us for it to be otherwise.

ALEXIS WRIGHT

Project Managers: Kent MacCarter & Rebecca Starford
Managing Editor: Kent MacCarter
Developmental Editors: Kent MacCarter & Ali Lemer
Copy Editor: Ali Lemer
ESL Editor: Kent MacCarter

PEN Melbourne is delighted to be a patron of *Joyful Strains*. The anthology reflects the vision of PEN International, which affirms that literature knows no frontiers, and urges writers to do their utmost to dispel race, class and national hatreds.

Published by Affirm Press in 2013
28 Thistlethwaite Street, South Melbourne
www.affirmpress.com.au

Text copyright © Kent MacCarter & Ali Lemer
All rights reserved. No part of this publication may be reproduced without prior permission of the publisher.

A Cataloguing-in-Publication entry is available from the catalogue of the National Library of Australia at www.nla.gov.au
ISBN 978-0-9873085-3-5

Cover design by Dean Gorissen, Room44
Proudly printed in Australia by Griffin Press

This project has been assisted by the Australian Government through the Australia Council, its arts funding and advisory body.

MAKING AUSTRALIA HOME

EDITED by KENT MacCARTER & ALI LEMER

10	**ARNOLD ZABLE**	
	Introduction	
19	**DMETRI KAKMI** *Turkey*	
	Night of the Living Wog	
32	**ALICE PUNG** *Cambodia*	
	Stealing from Little Saigon	
41	**MARIA TUMARKIN** *Russia*	
	The Beast, the Accent	
46	**MICHAEL SALA** *Netherlands*	
	Swarte Piet	
56	**MEG MUNDELL** *New Zealand*	
	Confessions of a Ditch-Jumper	
67	**PAOLA TOTARO** *Italy*	
	Pointing North	
78	**CHI VU** *Vietnam*	
	The Uncanny	
89	**MALLA NUNN** *Swaziland*	
	An Unanswered Prayer	
96	**AMY ESPESETH** *United States*	
	Staying Away	
106	**ROANNA GONSALVES** *India*	
	The Patron Saint of Excess Baggage	
117	**MICHELLE AUNG THIN** *Burma*	
	Backtracking	
124	**CHRIS FLYNN** *Ireland*	
	Gun for Hire	
134	**DIANE ARMSTRONG** *Poland*	
	Cracker Night	

142	**GHASSAN HAGE** *Lebanon*	
	On Other Belongings	
151	**OUYANG YU** *China*	
	When Shall We Get Back to Our Country?	
162	**DANNY KATZ** *Canada*	
	The Crappiest Refugee	
171	**MARK DAPIN** *United Kingdom*	
	Nineteen Eighty-Eight	
179	**DEBORAH CARLYON** *Papua New Guinea*	
	Hidden by the Dream	
189	**ADIB KHAN** *Bangladesh*	
	Here, There	
201	**ALI ALIZADEH** *Iran*	
	Sally	
211	**LILY YULIANTI FARID** *Indonesia*	
	The Range Hood and the Grease	
220	**JUAN GARRIDO-SALGADO** *Chile*	
	'I Have Three Wounds': Of Life, Love and Death	
232	**CATHERINE REY** *France*	
	To Make a Prairie it Takes a Clover and One Bee	
243	**SHALINI AKHIL** *Fiji*	
	Home and (Take)Away	
251	**VAL COLIC-PEISKER** *Croatia*	
	Deliberations of a Reasonably Domesticated Immigrant	
261	**HSU-MING TEO** *Malaysia*	
	Here and There and Over the Sea to Sky	
271	**SAMINA YASMEEN** *Pakistan*	
	Tape and Memory	

EDITORS' NOTE

Australia is deep in the throes of expanding multiculturalism. While newspaper ink and pixels are spilled daily in an attempt to make sense of its complex tangle of issues, literary responses to Australian immigration are far rarer. Never before has there been published a collection of the experiences and insights of expatriate authors responding personally to this question of Australian cultural diversity – not simply as grist for the headlines or a panel on *Q&A*, but sharing the real effects of uprooting their lives to make Australia their home.

Joyful Strains reflects the ethnic diversity that has grown as swiftly in the arts as it has in the Australian national census. The writers in this anthology share their stories of migration – by turns harrowing and joyful, hilarious and profound – in bewitching detail. Their motivations for relocating to this 'lucky country', and how their native cultures add to and contrast against the dynamics of Australian life, are the essence of this book.

As expatriates ourselves, we know what it means to tear away from bonds of home and family to start over in a new country. Like this book's contributors, we too turned our lives upside down to move here, from New York City and Chicago – cities that have been inspirational destinations for people the world over for nearly two centuries. Coming from the United States – much like Australia, a nation built by the striving of immigrants, with a complex and difficult colonial history – we found ourselves thinking about the experience of expatriation, in not only our own lives, but those of others who faced far different experiences. How much harder is it, for example, for those who don't speak English fluently? How do other expats adjust to Australian life? How do things from daily trivialities to profoundly emotional events challenge expatriates' perceptions of 'home'?

We chose to move here, but many of the writers in this collection were not blessed with the same freedom. Although the title refers to 'expats', the terms 'refugee' or 'political exile' are more applicable to some of the contributors. Others were at the mercy of their parents' decisions.

We wanted to give native-born Australians an outsider's insight into their country. A national literature needs to encompass *all* Australian stories to truly reflect the modern nation we have become – no matter how we got here.

KENT MacCARTER *and* ALI LEMER

ARNOLD ZABLE

Introduction

Apart from Australia's Indigenous peoples, we are all descendants of expatriates. The title of the collection – with its sly allusion to the national anthem – is apt. For immigrants adjusting to a new life, the pendulum swings between joy and strain, and at the extremes between trauma and moments of elation. Making a home in a new country is a daunting task, unique in its trajectory for each individual who undertakes the journey.

When I envisage the emotional swings endured by my parents, the first image that comes to mind is of them making their way through the streets of Carlton to the community centre, for a night of Yiddish theatre. There was a sense of celebration in the crowded foyer. Many present were survivors of the horrors of war. They spent the weekdays in factories, milk bars, at market stalls, on building sites, and in embryonic businesses, but on this night they felt at home. The pendulum swings to the opposite extreme, and I relive my mother's rages at the fate of her murdered loved ones, compounded by her longing for the Polish–Jewish community she had been a part of pre-war. Her rages were visceral and disturbing.

They spoke of intense isolation, of lost hope and meaning.

I have witnessed many examples of emotional swings in recent years in my encounters with recently arrived asylum seekers. Iraqi Amal Basry survived the SIEV X sinking on 19 October 2001, by clinging to a body for over twenty hours. Three hundred and fifty-three men, women and children drowned on that ill-fated voyage en route to Christmas Island. Amal's trauma was compounded by a system of temporary visas that perpetuated her state of limbo. On hearing the news she had received her permanent visa, she exclaimed, 'I am a free woman in a free country.' Yet almost every night she would awaken from a suffocating dream of being back in the water.

Years after arriving as a child with her family in flight from Vietnam, Chi Vu writes of her sense of awe at the consequences of having been a refugee: 'my family and I could have all easily died at sea, no problem, no trace, unable to be found, as was the fate of up to half a million of our contemporaries.'

Yet there are saving graces, strange new hybrids: my mother, a performer of Yiddish songs pre-war — English was her sixth language — singing *When Irish Eyes Are Smiling*, as she goes about her household chores. And comical incidents, inspired by seemingly trivial misunderstandings. Soon after their arrival, Vu's family are perplexed by the NO STANDING sign at the bus stop outside their Melbourne hostel; her father is dismayed at the thought they had risked their lives for a more repressive regime than they had fled.

Vu, like other authors featured in this anthology, is both a skilled writer and an expatriate. The twenty-seven pieces include, as JM Coetzee stated after reading this collection, 'gems of the memoirist's art'. The secret lies in the detail, in the writers' alertness to the textures of everyday life and their contemplation of their experiences.

There are 'moments of being', as Virginia Woolf called them, that enable a reader to comprehend the fluctuating perceptions of home experienced by expatriates. Ghassan Hage's seminal essay pivots on such a moment. While standing in the unkempt backyard of the Bathurst house in which his Lebanese grandparents once lived, Hage discerns 'three unmistakable forms: a fig tree, an olive tree and a pomegranate tree – the holy Mediterranean trinity'. He derives from this episode an expected sense of belonging, one that shifts his sense of Australia beyond its compromised colonial past.

Arriving from England in 1988 as a vacationer, Mark Dapin immediately relishes the chance to reinvent himself and rewrite the 'wasted years'. His life proves far more successful than he could have imagined, 'but I'd needed to leave home to make it happen. I had to leave myself behind.' Chris Flynn is able to shake off his typecast Irish past and launch 'the new, sleek, bald version of Flynn 2.0 into the void'. While the move from rural Swaziland to suburban Perth was a confronting experience for Malla Nunn, her parents quickly saw 'what Australia lacked: the signs posted at every junction telling individuals of every race group where to stand, where to eat and where to sleep.' Roanna Gonsalves reflects upon the intermittent horrors inflicted upon minority groups in India that drove her family to seek refuge elsewhere. Yet she is also acutely sensitive to a history of race conflict in the new country, and in choosing to make Australia home, sees herself as complicit in perpetuating the inequality between Indigenous and non-indigenous people.

After decades of moving between China and Australia, Ouyang Yu defines himself as 'a wandering expatriate'. He draws on *piaobo*, a Chinese verb that denotes a state of drifting-anchoring. 'When shall I get back to my country?' he asks. 'Probably never, because I am already in my country, the one in my mind.' Bangladeshi Adib Khan coins the expression, 'polygamy of place', and celebrates the knowledge gained from living simultaneously in two countries. In a similar vein, Burmese–Canadian expatriate Michelle Aung Thin is 'well versed in seeing two places at once – West and East; new and old; bog-ordinary and impossibly exotic. But double vision is also double-edged. When you see double, committing to one place isn't so easy.'

In a daring move, Catherine Rey burns her bridges in forsaking France, mid-life, for Australia. She contemplates the challenges of living in two tongues and discovers her writer's voice in a synthesis between the two. Michael Sala is also pulled in two directions. When in Australia, his family focused on what they saw as the cultural depth of Holland, but when they returned to Holland, they recalled the open space and potential for reinvention in the new land. Meg Mundell has made a good life here, and professes a fondness for the adopted country. But she remains homesick for New Zealand and is disturbed by the dismissive attitudes Australians have towards Kiwi culture. Deborah Carlyon casts a critical eye on both her Papua New Guinean homeland and Australia, and the uneasy relationship their men have with women. In her riveting tale, Amy Espeseth reveals the specific reason she is afraid to return from her adopted Australia to rural Wisconsin. Her predicament is compounded by the physical distance between the two locations, and the sense of isolation it fosters.

The noisy, smoky wet kitchens of Makassar in Indonesia present a sharp contrast to the kitchens that Lily Yulianti Farid encounters in Australia. Her nostalgia is tempered by the increasing range of homeland ingredients that can be obtained in the cosmopolitan city that Melbourne has become. It takes several journeys between Australia and Fiji before Shalini Akhil finds her place in a Melbourne suburb that caters to the tastes of many lands. Observing food markets in the same western suburbs, Alice Pung witnesses a harsher reality – the ongoing struggle to make good, and the price the immigrant pays to feel secure. The market appears exotic to cultural tourists, but they 'do not see the missing fingers from meat slicers, the feet ruined by vats of hot oil accidentally spilled, the hacking coughs from inhaling the floating mites of polyester fibres'.

While depicting the merciless taunts and brutalities of the schoolyard, Dmetri Kakmi finds solace in his television heroes. Kakmi has a talent for seeing the world through the eyes of the immigrant child he once was. Iranian Ali Alizadeh is bullied by the schoolyard mob in regional NSW. Racism and xenophobia thwart his efforts to feel at home. His burden is compounded by the torments of unrequited love, and the conflicting pressures of alternating between the cultures of school and home.

In contrast, Diane Armstrong's and Hsu-Ming Teo's childhood transitions to new lives are made bearable by small kindnesses. Both are acutely aware of the freedom they experience in Australia, as compared to, in Armstrong's case, the horrors she had endured as a hidden Jewish child in Poland, and in Teo's case, the strictures of her Malaysian childhood. 'He was my favourite teacher,' she writes of the guitar-strumming Mr Lyne, 'because he showed me that I didn't have to be afraid.' Samina Yasmeen feels unexpectedly at home when she arrives from Pakistan as a student in 1979. But after the collapse of the Twin Towers on 9/11, an unfamiliar 'darkness rolled overhead', causing a radical shift in the way she is perceived. For Paola Totaro, school life as an Italian kid in a Sydney neighbourhood in the early 1970s was a 'jarring mix of joy and trepidation'.

In her challenging essay, Maria Tumarkin expresses fatigue at being defined by her immigrant status years after settling in Australia: 'I am a post-migrant, even though the beast, the accent, is still there – thick and sticky on my off days, impossible to peel off.' Val Colic-Peisker is also tired of the question, 'Where do you come from?' After return visits home, she becomes less enamoured of status-conscious Croatia, and a fan of Australia's laissez-faire attitudes to expression and dress. Canadian-born Danny Katz resorts to biting satire in expressing his fatigue with the political correctness that can characterise the immigrant story.

Yet the story matters. It matters a lot. The last words of my introduction go to Juan Garrido-Salgado. As refugees from Pinochet's brutal dictatorship, Garrido-Salgado and his family struggle to adjust to suburban Adelaide. Slowly they find kindred spirits who share their passion for social justice. They learn of the dispossession upon which the new land was founded and begin to connect with Indigenous peoples. They visit Baxter detention centre and see the injustices inflicted upon a new generation of asylum seekers. Through sharing their concern for the outcast they find common ground. Juan concludes: 'This is now my land too.'

PEN Melbourne is delighted to be a patron of this collection. The writers in this anthology offer insights that reflect the aspirations and vision of PEN International. As the PEN charter affirms, literature knows no boundaries. PEN was founded on the premise that the written word is precious.

Good writing transports us across borders and cultures. In sharing our tales, we come to recognise both our differences and what unites us. There cannot be one without the other. In acknowledging our uniqueness, and the varied ways in which succeeding generations of expatriates have adjusted to the new country, we discover what we have in common. The specific story mirrors our humanity.

DMETRI KAKMI

Night of the Living Wog

When my family emigrated from Turkey to Australia in 1971, the aeroplane flew from Istanbul to Athens and then, after a lengthy stopover, from Athens to Melbourne. In those days flights landed briefly in Bahrain and Karachi before nosing south. It was a monstrous flight for a nine-year-old who had not been inside a flying machine before, let alone heard of the Arab Emirates or Pakistan. I dare say it was with relief that I stepped onto the tarmac at Tullamarine airport, but I can't remember any of it. All I recall is that one minute I was on board an Olympic Airlines conveyance and the next in a stinking hot, overly bright and incredibly flat suburb in Melbourne's north, a world away from hilly Tenedos, the Aegean island from whence my family hailed.

As ethnic Greeks who had been born and raised in Turkey, my parents were excited by the prospect of the Athens stopover: it would be their first visit to Greece. The ancient capital was for them a dewdrop of heaven – an oasis of peace, calm and tranquility – that promised an end to persecution and the beginning of acceptance to the Hellenic tribe.

My parents were in for a shock. It did not occur to either one that they were going from one ideology to another: Turkish nationalism to the Greek military junta. They were crushed when airport security took one look at our Turkish passports, decided we were spies and quickly ferried us to a hotel, where we stayed until our next flight out. Two guards were stationed in the corridor to make sure the traitorous Greco-Turks did not escape and plunder state secrets.

A mysterious box occupied a corner of the hotel room. It had four spindly legs and a black screen in which flitted our anxious reflections. As sluggish rain fell out of a grey sky and seagulls landed on the windowsill to study the inmates, Mum and Dad, my younger sister and I skulked around the box, wondering about its purpose. No one was brave enough to approach it and test its capabilities. Finally, I opened the door and asked one of the guards. He came in and with the flick of a wrist switched on the television.

I sat on the edge of the bed and watched an episode of what I later learnt was a show called *I Love Lucy*, dubbed in Greek. Lucille Ball's antics made us laugh and eased the tension. A few days later, in 15 Brooke Street, Northcote, my mother's younger sister switched on a similar contraption in her lounge room and there was the same shrill woman. This time she spoke fluent English.

'Goodness,' I thought. 'The crazy Greek lady flew with us to Australia and learnt to speak English in record time.'

Alone in my aunt's lounge room, I walked up to the television and peeked behind it. Nothing but a black cable connected to the wall. There were no miniature tree-lined streets, no houses and no people engaged in frantic activity. And yet sound emerged from within, and when I touched the plastic backing, heat and a mystifying vibration enticed my hand. I crossed myself. 'Mother of God.' The wooden box was bigger on the inside than it was on the outside. 'How is this possible?' I dared not ask my two younger cousins, who had grown up in Melbourne and took these marvels for granted.

The answer came a day or so later with my first episode of *Doctor Who*. The television was a kind of Tardis, bigger on the inside than on the outside. Through a confluence of technology and magic, it contained worlds within worlds and possessed unlimited power and knowledge. In this manner began a lifelong love affair with a multiform technology that was akin to the all-seeing, all-knowing eye of Zeus.

⬥

The first two years were bewildering and unsettling for a boy who turned ten the week he arrived in Melbourne. By all accounts, I was a peasant for whom life was circumscribed by the sea, and by narrow experience and education. The island from which the family came was primitive and, despite its geographical location at the crossroads of two continents, isolated. Our homes had no running water, and electricity was reserved for street lighting. Most people were illiterate. The one telephone in the village resided in the post office, and transport was by horse and donkey. Cars were rare, miraculous machines that accompanied visiting foreigners. Music and news came via battery-operated radio, and the cinema was a black-and-white enchantment.

Such were the circumstances of our modest lives, and it is almost impossible to convey to a city dweller how utterly overwhelming it was to suddenly find one's self in a thrumming megalopolis. Here electricity was the life-blood that pulsed in the veins of every street and home. Cars, trams, buses and trains were pressed into harried service to convey the restless hordes that thronged the streets at all hours. Noise, after the vast silence of the island, was the heartbeat and the breath of a ravenous beast whose hunger could not be appeased.

As my brain ticked away at the problem of how to locate myself within the city's sprawl, I realised that the answer had stared me in the face all along: television.

This fabulous invention was no mere abstraction. For someone who was used to living in his head, the images presented on screen were more real and contained more truth than reality. Discovering television when I did shifted the ground beneath my feet and influenced my life, even forcing me to reassess cherished beliefs. For instance, I had seen *Mutiny on the Bounty* with Marlon Brando in Turkey, and because the handsome man spoke

Turkish, I presumed the actor was a Turk. In the same year I had interpreted the shuffling flesh-eaters in *Night of the Living Dead* as Turkish zombies come to feast on peaceable Greek farmers. But when I saw the same dramas on a television in a suburban Melbourne home, I realised that the movies I had enjoyed in my homeland were made in Australia. (America had yet to enter my consciousness.)

Television was no mere entertainment to while away the hours. To my malleable brain it was a benevolent tool of the government, an electronic medium that inducted new arrivals in local rituals and habits. I reasoned that if one acted on the lessons imparted by the all-knowing box, one would assimilate very quickly. From a distance of forty years, I can report that my schoolyard enemies were neither impressed nor intimidated when I folded my arms in front of me and blinked to make them disappear, like Major Nelson's genie did in *I Dream of Jeannie*. Batman's *KAPOW!* proved to be infinitely more effective.

The act of watching expanded, rather than limited, my world view. Each afternoon, as I watched *Prince Planet*, *Gigantor*, *Flipper* and *Skippy*, it seemed that the box held the key to this land of blond people who invariably possessed iridescent blue eyes and who inevitably felt the urge to hurt those that did not. They were as intimidating as the nationalists we left behind, whom my parents wanted to forget. The black people (who were said to live behind a fence) had yet to make an appearance. Even so, I felt that, should I meet any, I would have more in common with them than with the mean-eyed, thin-lipped pale-skins who thought an olive skin was cause for alarm and revulsion.

Dislocation and discombobulation were emblematic of my first years in Melbourne. Erasing Tenedos from my mind and converting Victoria's capital into my new mental space became a psychological and metaphysical imperative. The turning point came with the discovery of a local police drama called *Division 4*. As I watched spunky Terence Donovan and Ted Hamilton restore law and order to mean streets that were obliquely, haphazardly connected to avenues I traversed on the way to school or the milk bar, I began to orient myself within a larger urban framework. The tram that trundled down Rucker's Hill in Northcote went through a variety of suburbs to the city: the place of tall buildings. There was no reason to fear the suburban sprawl in between – it was merely a collection of districts connected by a network of roads and railway lines that were open to all citizens.

In this manner a great map unfolded inside my head and, quite suddenly, the pin dropped. I saw myself astride a Melways map with all Melbourne's heretofore hidden and admittedly scant secrets revealed. In this manner, Tenedos and Melbourne combined to form a complicated inner landscape, a nebulous place that shifted in and out of focus according to my moods.

It is said that we find the teacher we deserve. The centaur Chiron mentored Achilles, son of the nymph Thetis. Mentor, son of Alcimus, educated Telemachus, son of Odysseus. It is appropriate, then, that someone who lived inside a television set should have educated Dmetri Kakmi, son of Vangel Kakmioğlu. My teacher was Catweazle, a medieval wizard who travels through time to twentieth-century England, where he befriends a young boy. It was largely through the eyes of Geoffrey Bayldon's comic creation that I came to grips with technological innovation.

I was so bamboozled by everyday electrical appliances that, for the longest time, I felt like my confused comrade Catweazle, lurching from one comic shock-horror moment to the next. The first time a slice of burnt bread popped out of the toaster I screamed, leaped back, and then skulked over to inspect the machine's innards with a butter knife. When told to take a bath, I undressed and stood in the bathtub, waiting for water to magically pour on me. I was under the impression that the car knew when to turn on the indicator lights because it could read the driver's mind. Everything was an occasion for immense study and contemplation – I did not even know that toilets were to be flushed after use.

Despite my younger cousins' mirth, I took Catweazle's antics seriously. As he became acquainted with electricity – or 'electrickery', as he called it – I realised that his mind had the same fluid admixture of superstition and science as mine; his childlike curiosity, caution and willingness to learn through trial and error mirrored my own advent into puzzling modernity. By turns brave and cowardly, he was the perfect vehicle for vicarious experience, and to this day I am grateful to him for seemingly risking himself on my behalf.

⬥

Anonymity is impossible in a Turkish village, privacy an incomprehensible concept. Neither one of these words existed for me until I came to Australia. Fellow Tenedians knew you as well as you knew them. Your identity – the comprehension of who you were on a cellular level – was determined by your place in the social hierarchy. You were not a separate entity. You belonged first to the family, then to the community.

Melbourne, with its jealously guarded backyard culture, was built to keep people apart. The requirement of privacy dominated its architecture and the topographical layout of streets. That was reflected on a microcosmic level by estranged families and neighbours who kept to themselves. We came from a place where every citizen had a role to play, but Melbourne appeared to have no concept of civic wholeness, nor indeed did it make a distinction between aloneness and loneliness. For once Catweazle's example did not suit me. He, a wizard dedicated to arcane knowledge, chose to be a hermit. I, on the other hand, was a child who wanted to get out of the house and mix with kids his own age. The dilemma was that the rules were different in this country and I did not know how to interpret them. A sense of desolation swept through me when it finally dawned on me that Melbourne had no recognisable human network in which to place myself. For the first time in my life, I was alone and had to make my own way in the world.

The situation was exacerbated by the fact that in Turkey I was Greek in the home and Turk on the street. Easily conversing in both languages, I happily identified as Greco–Turk; to this day I feel more kinship to my country of birth than to its Hellenic counterpart across the Aegean. Yet the minute we embarked on our Australian adventure, my parents felt the need to assert their absolute Greekness, going so far as to send their two children to Greek school in the evenings and on weekends. 'We are Greek,' I was told. Given how Hellenes treated us during our short stay in Athens, this sat very badly with me.

Things got worse when I enrolled at Westgarth Primary School. After filling in the appropriate paperwork, the headmaster gazed at me across the large desk and said: 'In Australia we can't pronounce your name. From now on your name is Jim.'

This resulted in an existentialist dilemma. From then on, not only did I not know where I was but I was no longer who I had been. In essence, the peasant boy was stripped of place and identity and left to wander a no man's land straight out of *The Twilight Zone*. Dmetri was familiar to me; I knew him well enough. Who was Jim? I did not know what to make of this half-Greek, half-Australian boy, and had to invent him from the ground up. This led to the creation of a malleable persona that could be made to fit the mood and circumstance. Jim was whomever he needed to be in order to survive; in time, his presence in Dmetri's body led to an internalised schism.

Over the course of the next dozen years, Jim rejected his Greek–Turkish heritage and forgot how to speak both languages. Dmetri crouched in a corner and grew angry and resentful. To cope, I began to refer to myself in the third person – 'Jim likes this but Dmetri doesn't,' I'd say. People thought I was either bonkers or pretentious. It was not until the age of twenty-two, when I jettisoned Jim from my body and reverted to strictly being Dmetri, that I felt comfortable in my skin. Even then I had to contend with charges that I was adopting an ethnic persona that was not rightfully mine, so I could be more interesting and exotic.

Inspired by Lucille Ball's astounding linguistic capabilities, I commandeered English six months after my arrival. I was so accomplished that my classmates thought I was pretending to be 'a new Australian', and beat me for supposedly duping them. Despite my best efforts to fit in, I was called 'wog' and 'dago', and was bashed in and out of the schoolyard. It was not until I opened a boy's head with a Coke bottle and someone else's face with a rusty old clock found in a gutter that the bullies stayed away. Violence, the only language those around me seemed to understand, became my *modus operandi*.

As primary school ended and high school began, it dawned on me that I was, in essence, an outsider, a skinny bookworm who flitted ghost-like on the periphery, watching and trying to curry favour with the boys he feared and admittedly desired, without understanding what that entailed.

Around this time I discovered the Universal and Hammer horror movies that screened on Channel 10. These bone-chilling phantasmagorias from the crypt satisfied my gothic sensibility and gave a face to the operatic fantasies of violent revenge that filled my head. Movies such as *Dr Jekyll and Mr Hyde*, *The Phantom of the Opera*, *The Mummy* and *Frankenstein* provided endless hours of glee and, as a natural course of action, intensified my identification with the monster. For a teenager who believed himself to be ugly, disgusting and unwanted, the rampaging undead, bursting from graves, symbolised his own outcast state even as their exploits offered him a pathetic grab at power and control. It hardly mattered that the fiends were annihilated before the end credits. There was comfort in the knowledge that they returned next week to wreak further havoc on their tormentors.

My inclination to violence dropped significantly after watching a horror movie. These metaphoric fables from the unconscious taught me that force is not a viable answer; if anything, its application exacerbates a situation. After what we had lived through in Turkey, brute force was the last thing I wanted in my life. These movies also taught me to identify with the underdog. To this day, I despise Dracula's nemesis Van Helsing, and I understand – though hardly condone – the kids responsible for the Columbine massacre. I often wanted to do the same to my classmates.

The novel *Carrie* was a cornerstone of these years. Reading Stephen King's tale of bullying and bloody vengeance for the first time was like opening the pages to my own autobiography. When Carrie suffered, I suffered. When she cried, I cried. And I fully comprehended Flaubert's meaning when he wrote, '*Madame Bovary, c'est moi.*' I felt the same way about Carrie White. My love affair with her intensified when my father took me to see Brian De Palma's film version at the Preston drive-in. This extreme identification reached a peak one Friday afternoon in careers counselling. 'What do you want to be when you leave school, Jim?' the teacher asked. 'Carrie White, sir,' I replied. Maybe that's why I have not been invited to any Northcote High School reunions.

Power and desire fused into one, and by the time I left high school I was finding my role models in the most unlikely characters. *My Favorite Martian*, *The Munsters*, *The Addams Family*, Captain Gregg from *The*

Ghost and Mrs Muir, *Batman*, Endora from *Bewitched*: they all populated my imagination and fed my dreams. These gleeful oddballs put the lie to conformism. By inhabiting the fringes and revelling in individualism, they represented an underbelly that made a virtue of quiet and homely subversion. Their stratagem was clear enough: Be as outlandish as you like, just don't let others know what you're up to. Although I did not always agree with their stealth, they taught me to appreciate the freak inside.

♠

It is no overstatement to say that television saved my life. At a crucial point, its febrile electronic pulses guided me away from thin ice towards the greener pastures of Western life. Along the way this singular mode of communication adopted various angel-like guises – Lucille Ball, Catweazle, Doctor Who – and taught me the value of being true to one's self. Television even made some of life's awkward moments easier than they might have been without it. In Turkey, I could not have told my parents that I am attracted to men – life would have been a quiet misery of clandestine creeping around. Not so in Australia, where we were weaned on *Number 96* and *The Box*. Why, I still remember the day when my mother said: 'If Joan Collins in *Dynasty* can accept her gay son, so can I.'

ALICE PUNG
Stealing from Little Saigon

My mother knows a certain marketplace in Melbourne the same way some people know their own spouses. She comes from two generations of traders. She knows all the different ways to get around any market, how to coax, control, cajole and conquer: all the tricks of the trade. Our great-grandmother hawked boiled eggs on the streets of Phnom Penh, her own mother sold fried rice-and-chive cakes before Pol Pot came, and when they were exiled in Vietnam, my mother sold fabric in a Saigon stall.

This market is called the Little Saigon Market, and my mother shops here twice a week. If you walked inside and paid no heed to the outside world, you could very well be in Vietnam. It has white tiles on the floor, and a number of different stalls selling everything from durian cakes and roast ducks to jewellery and rice-bowl-shaped bras. There are also two large supermarkets of the non-chain variety selling fresh produce, including over five different types of mushroom – enoki, shiitake, oyster, Korean and standard brown. One of the supermarkets carries swimming, crawling seafood in tanks. In any other suburb, a market with this sort of fare would be considered an exotic place for gourmands, with the prices handwritten on squares of cardboard with neat black frames, beneath the one-sentence description of the obscure comestible. But not here. Here, you can get mangoes for three dollars a kilo.

The name says everything you need to know about the migrants who run the place – what era they come from, what government they were under before they left, and their nostalgic yearnings towards some point in the past. In many ways, our lives revolve around the marketplace, and from an outsider's view, our parents seem to be trying to replicate the patterns of their youth in Phnom Penh. These are people who bury gold in their backyards and buy three-day-old buns from the bakery. All their lives have been about sequestering things away so that no one can see how much they have, in case forces more powerful – governments, soldiers, the snaking coils of family nepotism gone poisonous – take what they have. Humility, hard work and an over-vigilant sense of privacy – that's what they now believe in.

However, the same values seem not to apply when it comes to scrutinising other people. One evening, my mother came home and told us about a woman in town whose husband was much older than her. My mother said she tried to keep out of things, but she couldn't help having ears. 'She's so young and she is looking after a decrepit old man,' the gossipmongers whispered to each other in the vegetable stall when they saw the wife leading her husband by the elbow and choosing tomatoes. In the jewellery stores when the wife came to sell off some gold to pay for her husband's most recent hospital bill, they talked. In the bank, when she was lining up with him to collect his pension, they whispered.

One day, the odd couple came to the electrical appliance store where my mother worked, to buy an iron. 'My son is moving to work in Bendigo this year,' the wife told my mother, and all who were within earshot. 'He's become a doctor.'

'What a smart son you have!' my mother exclaimed. All the while wondering, as they all did, *exactly how large a gap is there between you and your husband?*

'He's smart like his mother!' the old man chuckled. 'She was such a smart little girl. Did you know that when we were in the camp, she used to collect cola cans, and somehow she ended up making little chairs and tables from them.'

'We stayed for twelve years at the Thai refugee camp,' added his wife.

'Yes, and when the Red Cross white people and the Jesus white people came to set up their tents, they would be so charmed by her little tin furniture that they actually gave her some money for them! Hehehe.'

'Shut up, you.' She gave him a little push on his shoulder.

'Oi! Be careful you don't topple your old man over!'

'So, did you know each other at the camp?' my mother asked.

'We met at the camp,' the wife said.

'She was wandering around, like a little lost creature.'

'I was only twelve.'

'But as smart as a fox.'

'The Black Thieves smashed my parents,' said the wife – and of course my mother knew who the Black Thieves were, it was what they all called the Khmer Rouge in Cambodia – 'and then a cousin took me to the camp. He –' she pointed to her husband '– he was thirty years old. He had once worked for my parents back in Phnom Penh. He became my older brother. He looked after me when I was a small child in the camp for all those years, and so now it's my turn to look after him.'

It was then that my mother realised that the woman wasn't so young, and that her husband wasn't so old. Suffering had etched calligraphy lines of experience all over his face, and he had alleviated as much of his wife's hardships as he could, which is probably why she looked the way she did.

※

Recently, my mother told us that she had seen a small bout of shoplifting at one of the two supermarkets in Little Saigon. While my mother was trying to buy some spinach, there was a loud yell. My mother looked towards the nectarine trestle table and saw that a cleaver-wielding man, eyes popping like a *dybbuk*, had grabbed hold of the wrist of a petrified young Indian woman with a long braid down her back. 'Thief! Thief!' he hollered. He held up a clear plastic bag containing a single mango. 'You haven't paid for this.'

'Yes, I have.'

'*Where* did you pay for this?'

'Over there.' She pointed to the furthermost counter.

'That's not our counter!'

The stalls were set up in such haphazard fashion that you could not tell where one market began and the other ended. If this was your first time, you would think that it was one enormous market, until you started to notice the counters.

Yet my mother had seen the young woman walking around the market with the mango in her bag for a while. The man led her to the correct counter, still clinging to the cleaver which he used to cut open nectarines for customers to taste. 'Did she pay for this?'

'No,' yelled the cashier woman, 'she did not come here to pay.'

'We call the police!' declared the cleaver-wielding man.

The young Indian woman's eyebrows knotted and she looked like she was about to cry.

'Please don't call the police,' she begged, opening up her purse, 'I pay for it.'

'We call the police. You pay for it now.'

She took out some coins and handed them to the cashier.

'Twenty dollars, or we call police.'

'Twenty dollars?'

'Twenty dollars.'

'For one mango?'

'For you steal.'

'But I don't have twenty dollars.'

'Then wait here, we call police.' Grabbing her wrist, he took out his mobile phone with one hand.

'Okay, okay I pay.'

The marketplace is a law unto itself, where moral cause-and-effect accumulates interest. The mores are simple, the sort of universal laws that one would find within the first ten or so precepts of every major faith and culture: don't steal, don't lie, don't cheat. A rigid and unassailable sense of morality comes with a certain level of comfort, perhaps: a conviction that life will not change, or that God will not blink or turn his face away. But these were not my mother's convictions. She had never believed in a compassionate God. She came from a country where women's throats were cut with palm leaves and coconut juice had been used in intravenous drips as a blood substitute. Where people were still scrambling for food scraps on the floor. The kind of stealing my mother witnessed was not the happy frisson of high-school hijinks.

She knew it for what it was – it was a secret, this shame. Even though the trestle tables were so laden with fruit that every evening at six o'clock the market workers would stuff plastic bags and sell them for two dollars each, the Indian girl wasn't supposed to be trying to smuggle out that lump of fruit without having paid for it, just as my mother knew she wasn't supposed to have lied at the refugee camp to smuggle a seed of a different sort out. She was eight months pregnant with me when she arrived in Australia, and the only way she could get on that plane was to lie and say that she was only four months.

Perhaps it was similar to the sort of shame that made my parents afraid to ask for things, even from fifteen-year-olds behind the counter at McDonald's; they always got us to ask for the sweet-and-sour sauce for our nuggets, always berated us for our sullen reluctance. It was the petty avarice of the poor, and punished even more harshly by the migrants who had been here longer and who had achieved the enviable 'permanent resident' status, because this thievery reminded them of who they used to be, how they used to think and, occasionally, what they used to do.

♠

I had seen it one time myself, when I was leading an interviewer and filmmaker through Footscray Market, two blocks away from Little Saigon. Filmmakers who feel like they need an authentic visa into Footscray and the world of these migrants and their markets sometimes ask me to be their passports. Their genuine sense of decency cringes at filming poverty, but led through the streets by a loquacious local guide, this suddenly becomes an adventure akin to those they had when they backpacked through Vietnam or Laos. I am the link between what is foreign – the market – and what is familiar – my made-in-Australia roots and no Oriental accent.

That day, there was yelling in the middle of the fruit section. 'She come-a do this every week!' hollered the Mediterranean fruit stall owner, who had his hand firmly on the vinyl-covered trolley of an old, stooped-over Asian grandma. He flung open the flap of her trolley to reveal a bunch of bananas and some potatoes. 'Come see! Come see!' he beckoned to the film crew. He wanted to catch the culprit on film, even though the documentary was about something else.

'Have pity on me,' the old woman cried in Cantonese, lifting up her trouser leg, 'my leg hurts.' Sure enough, her leg was bandaged from the sockless foot to the mid-calf. By then, a small circle of onlookers had formed around the Greek fruitier, the old-lady pilferer and her trolley.

'Here, here,' said one woman, handing the market owner five dollars, 'take this! Take this! I pay for her.'

'No want your money!' He pushed the note aside. 'You no understand, she come-a do this every week!' He beckoned to the cameraman. 'Quick put camera here!' he directed, as if he were running the show.

We quietly made our exit, leaving the little circle to disperse itself. As we walked away, I realised this: there I was, with a camera crew and books and words, and I knew that the people whose worlds I wrote about would never read my books, and the people who read my books would never fully inhabit these worlds, even though they have already begun to populate them. And when they do, increasing the property prices of those already living in Footscray, they will make the existing residents very happy because now they will be able to purchase a house-and-land package in the newly opened manicured feats of urban planning that lie just a Toyota Camry drive away from the countryside. And Mr and Ms Market Owner will at last be able to move away from the hollering hot masses of fruit-pilfering new arrivals.

So I show my film crew strange fruit, and hope they quickly forget about the incident with the old lady. I show them how to dip slices of sour mango in dishes of salt and chilli. They look in astonishment at the cleaver-wielding hecklers. And then I take them to a pho restaurant for lunch.

I don't mention how housewives will heave and clutch their hearts over being short-changed ten cents. I never mention the young Indian woman who once put a single mango in a plastic bag without paying for it. At the end of the day, they can leave and marvel over the interesting cultural tour. They do not see the missing fingers from meat slicers, the feet ruined by vats of hot oil accidentally spilled, the hacking coughs from inhaling the floating mites of polyester fibres.

The marketplace is a front, the final face of our lives – the most charismatic, enterprising and proud. And the most extraordinary thing the filmmakers will take away from the day, the only true thing I will disclose about my mother's market, and the one thing they will write about in the newspapers with wonder, is that it is possible to buy mangoes for three dollars a kilo.

MARIA TUMARKIN

The Beast, the Accent

A man I was once married to back in the previous century – speaking, some time after the marriage was over, from one of Europe's megalopolises – called Australia 'a nation of sunken ships'. And to me, for whom, by that point, he wished little else, he wished an easy and swift escape. *Run*, he said, *Maria, run*.

He got to me then. (I got to him too, making sure he missed out on Australian citizenship: my most patriotic, most spiteful, action ever.)

Sunken. Not even sinking.

Ira Glass, from the indispensable *This American Life* radio show, said in an interview once that many of his fellow Americans had a childhood story at the ready to explain to others, and invariably to themselves – who they are and how they've come to be. I have my immigrant stories for that same purpose. Most migrants do. I am bored by mine. Feels ridiculous to pull them out, like hanging out long-since-dry washing. It's been twenty-two years.

New migrants come – they are new, and I am old; an old dog – and I see them, carless, at bus and tram stops with plastic supermarket bags cutting into their fingers. Last year I saw hundreds, *with* cars, at the Oakleigh branch of VicRoads the day before their registration was due, coming up to the ticket dispenser in the corner, the one that places you in queues, and peering into its screen like they were newborn kittens, listening hard to the instructions given by the voice in the machine. Not for the faint-hearted, that voice: so patient, so polite. Diabolically incomprehensible too – like this country all round.

I am a professional translator, one with a stamp. New migrants come to me – they are new, and I am old; old at being new – with their birth certificates and degree certificates and divorce certificates, with their recommendation letters from ballet academies and oil rigs. I translate statutory declarations from Russian women whose Australian husbands thought they were procuring themselves model Russian wives, wives unspoilt by all the gender equality bullshit, and the husbands (lovely guys, some of them) on discovering that this was not, or not *totally*, the case, went all kinds of berserk.

I translate declarations from men too, screwed dry by my female compatriots. It makes me wonder if mixed marriages are doomed, especially when you bring a person in from another place to marry them. I think a lot about mixed marriages, partly because as WH Auden said – 'Any marriage, happy or unhappy, is infinitely more interesting than any romance' – and partly because the happy and enduring mixed marriage, the kind I don't get to see in my little bureau of dysfunction and demise, seems to me the true test of multiculturalism. Can it work? Does it last? Is it for real?

I think a lot, too, about being new, now that I am anything but; about coming to a place where you have no past, no one remembers you, nothing is in its place. That feeling of everything – the distance between earth and sky, the smell of sweat on passers-by, the sound of water lunging out of a tap, the way people spread their bodies on trams – being not the way you've always, unthinkingly, known it to be.

Are there five stages of the expat experience, as once believed we had with grief? (A dogma well past its prime, yes, challenged to smithereens by now – but a not entirely irrelevant point of comparison?)

Actually, I have a better question: how come the whole idea of culture shock seems so very beige now, so domesticated, as if the 'shock' in culture shock is a piquant little jolt, good for circulation, edifying even?

I see shock – a fish-out-of-water convulsing shock – on new arrivals' faces. I have been in Australia too long to feel it. But I remember how it feels: looking into your new life is like staring at the sun; it burns your retina. There are moments when half of Australia feels this shock, not the full brunt, just enough to count, to shake us off our chairs – the moment in December 2010, for instance, when an asylum-seeker boat crashed into cliffs off Christmas Island, sinking within our field of vision, and we watched Christmas Islanders watch

children cling to bits of boat wreckage, and drown. We
– alive. They, children and adults – dead. Have you seen
those images?

'A nation of sunken ships,' the man who didn't like
Australia called us. Sunken. Not even sinking.

'Australia is a good place to retire to.' He said that too.
I remember hating him for it. Maybe I even hung the
phone up on him. I hope I did. But people, as you know,
talk like this about Australia, even people who don't
have many places to immigrate to. They say Australia is
slow, smug and provincial – thin on history, too sheltered
for its own good, a country without energy, or much
imagination. People run from Australia, you know, even
first-generation migrants.

A young man from Somalia, a multilingual son of
a diplomat, drove me home from the airport in a taxi
recently. He said people in Australia can't drive and turn
too aggressive behind the wheel because there are not
enough cars on Australian roads. 'You don't,' he said,
'get a chance to get good because you are never humbled
by the flows of traffic, by its self-organising logic, by
the lessons it has in store for you. And so you are all
impatience and rage and no humility.' He was new here,
this young man from Somalia. He had sharp eyes for this
country, and an analytical bent. He made me remember
how it was to be constantly itching with bewilderment,
to compulsively be doing 'compare and contrast', to
start falling for this country, loving it, while remaining
unreconciled to it.

I am old at being here, very old. I have told my immigrant stories – good old immigrant 'schtick' – many times already, have written them up into books, have milked them for laughs, have turned them into tiny poignant fables. Twenty-two years... 'Come on!' (Not WH Auden this time – Lleyton Hewitt.) I am not a migrant anymore.

I am a post-migrant, even though the beast, the accent, is still there – thick and sticky on my off days, impossible to peel off. The Australian Bureau of Statistics says 44 per cent of Australians are either born overseas or have at least one foreign-born parent. That makes me as statistically average as they come. Nothing to see here. Keep on moving.

Now, it's only when I see a person who is new to being here that something inside me is triggered, a feeling of not quite being able to arrive. I know in my head that this, right here, is the shore, the coveted firm ground under my feet, but when I look around (and I strain... and strain) all I can see is the otherworldly blueness of the unending sea.

MICHAEL SALA

Swarte Piet

As a kid in Holland, I didn't look forward to the coming of Santa Claus but of Sinterklaas – Saint Nicholas – who arrived by steamboat from Spain, and left presents on Saint Nicholas Eve; the night of 5 December. Sinterklaas was more imposing than Santa Claus: he rode a horse and dressed like a bishop in ceremonial gear, the white gown overlapped by the deep red of his mantle, a gold cross emblazoned on his mitre. He also carried a hefty-looking bishop's staff. He was a middleman for God, and I knew where to put him in the scheme of things, but he wasn't half as interesting as the servant who walked alongside his horse holding the reins – the Moor, Swarte Piet. Black Peter.

I didn't know what a Moor was. I didn't know that Moors had once transformed Spain into the most advanced part of Europe. I didn't know that the most famous Moor in the English language, Othello, had for centuries been strangling his Venetian wife in theatres and playhouses all over the world. But in my town, Bergen Op Zoom, far from Amsterdam, nearly everyone I encountered – apart from my Greek–Cypriot father –

had pale skin. A man like Swarte Piet, with such *black* skin and black curly hair, stood out. Especially when he was dressed like a Renaissance page, with a bright feather sweeping down from the brim of his hat. If you were bad, it was said that he gave you a bundle of birch twigs as a warning that he might beat you. If you were *really* bad, so one story went, he threw you in a sack and abducted you to the wilds of Spain.

But at the same time, with a chaotic energy that could have put Santa Claus to shame, he carried Saint Nicholas' sack full of gifts and distributed his sweets. In the lead-up to Saint Nicholas Eve, the Moor roamed neighbourhoods and schools. We didn't know that he was there until he hammered on the door with his fist. Then he'd open the door and hurl in handfuls of confectionery that bounced off walls and furniture and scattered along the floor. All I'd see was a flash of his hand. I'd scramble around on hands and knees with the other children, picking up the sweets and stuffing as many of them into my pockets as I could: biscuit pebbles scented with spices; sponge-like candy figures; liquorice in all shapes and sizes and colours, all warmed by my skin.

My most enduring memory of Saint Nicholas Eve happened not in Holland but in Australia, not in a snow-covered winter, but at the height of summer. The five of us – my stepfather, my mother, my brothers and me – hadn't seen Holland for three years. We were living in Queensland, crammed into an apartment block beside a caravan park in a stark, sparsely populated place called

Bribie Island. It was hot during the day, and windless and humid at night. I'd stare at palm trees and saltbushes against the star-filled night sky and will them to life. They wouldn't move even a fraction.

Before Bribie Island, we'd been living in the coastal city of Newcastle, passing through a handful of suburbs there over the space of two-and-a-half years. I'd started school a handful of times too, but struggled to settle each time before we moved to the next neighbourhood. One day we packed the car and kept driving north until we came to Bribie Island, which was connected to the mainland by a long, narrow bridge. I didn't know why we'd moved there. There was never a clear aim to our travel from place to place – we usually moved to find new opportunities somewhere else. That was more or less what my mother told us, and she was usually the one who decided when and where we moved. My mother's decisions were not so much based on logic as feeling. After spending around six months on Bribie Island, she and my stepfather began packing up our goods into boxes and I knew that we were getting ready to move again.

In the vinyl record collection that my mother had brought with her from Holland was an album of Saint Nicholas songs. On 5 December, she put the album on the record player and we sat around the Christmas tree, a drier, sparser version of the dense, fragrant, fairytale trees my stepfather used to bring home from the plantations in Holland. The tree was done up with glittery, chocolate adornments that an aunt from Holland had sent over.

The ornaments would have stayed fresh in the Dutch winter, but had become misshapen in the Australian heat. I couldn't see that, though, in the evening light. The room, the way that my mother set it up, existed only in the illumination of flickering candles and pinprick tree lights. Anything might happen at its dim borders.

We stared up at the Christmas tree and the shadows between the lights and the pine needles and branches, and sang along with the album, hoping that our voices would be interrupted at some point by that hammering of Swarte Piet's fist on the door. It was a summoning ritual. We were as far from Holland as we'd ever been, but with the warm crackle of the album filling the living room and us singing along, attention focused on the Christmas tree, I found it easy to forget where we were.

My mother still has a picture of my older brother and me taken not long after this. We have left Australia and returned to Holland. We are sitting on a bed, grinning, two tanned boys with startlingly white teeth. The sun in Australia has called us to account, made our Cypriot skin reveal who we are. We've never looked more alike than at that moment, but it's an illusion. We sit side by side against a blank wall that renders us almost as silhouettes.

Much as I had been in Australia, I was a curiosity in the Dutch classroom. I discovered that I'd lost most of my original language. I was not a Dutch kid who'd returned home after time spent away, but a strange, dark, inarticulate boy from a far-off country. At the same time, my mother's family did not welcome her back with the open arms she'd imagined. Most of her ten siblings refused to see her. She was what she'd been when she left: a divorcee – they didn't care why – and nearly all of them, my grandmother included, still held it against her, and found ways of making her life hell.

My father, who still lived in that same Dutch town where he and my mother had married and divorced, desperately wanted to see my older brother. But he didn't want anything to do with me. I didn't entirely understand the reasons behind this rejection, but certain aspects were obvious to me. My brother was three years older. He had a history with my father that I didn't. He was also far more athletic, and adapted easily to the places we moved between. Then there was the fact that my brother and I had returned to different things. He had come back to a landscape of memories and people that he knew, while I'd come back to a country only sparsely illuminated by the fragmented impressions I'd had as a young child.

In the face of this, any sense that I'd had of Holland as some sort of place of origin – as home – quickly evaporated. The same must have happened for my mother. She began to remember all of the reasons why she'd left in the first place. She soon started talking about Australia in a different way: her regret in leaving it behind, her longing for what it offered, the space, the freedom, the way that people there weren't so bound up in the past. That only made my own sense of displacement worse, but I didn't really think of Australia as home, either. I never had. I just thought of home as being *some place else*.

I think that for everyone who leaves the place they grew up in, especially to go to another country, the place that is left behind forms a sort of architecture for memory, for the sense of self, whether they like it or not. Because I grew up moving between countries, that architecture is tangled and doesn't bear the image of one place, but of many, all at once. They came to seem not completely real to me, the places we moved through, even that one into which I had been born. Or perhaps it was *me* that wasn't real or defined. From place to place, I felt myself to be a passing impression, a shadow on the wall.

I had brief moments of blending in. After a couple of years of living in Holland, when I sang Sinterklaas songs with the other children, I began to forget how strange my accent sounded and became lost with everyone else in waiting for that booming impact of Swarte Piet's hand on the door. The anticipation that I felt at his imminent appearance held an undercurrent of anxiety, but it was an enlivening and reassuring sensation that made the world outside the room larger and the world inside cosier and smaller. I felt like I belonged on that side of the door. And then there was the fundamental instinct that all the children around me seemed to share: the giggling, blinkered greed with which we fell to our hands and knees and competed for the sweets scattering across the floor.

Apart from these moments, the sense of being outside of things set the tone for my childhood, wherever we lived, and it didn't just come from struggling to adapt as we moved between places and cultures. Mine wasn't simply an immigrant family, it was also a dysfunctional one, and the two are inseparable for me, both in my sense of the past and my sense of self. I cannot describe one without the other. Over the space of eight years, from my earliest memories – from the beginning of their marriage to its violent disintegration, as we moved from Holland to Australia, back to Holland and eventually back to Australia again – my mother's second husband became an increasingly overbearing presence in my life. When he lost his temper, he would pick me up by the hair; when I crossed my legs he would kick me under the table because he wanted me to be more of a man. As he became more miserable, his violence worsened.

My mother had married him in an act of desperation. She had married him to get away from her relatives – my grandmother, aunts and uncles – who lived in or around Bergen Op Zoom, and who had always oppressed her with their prejudices and intense religious dogma. Brought up in that family, my mother had developed a knack for bad relationships. Her first husband, my Greek Cypriot father, had also been abusive. When she'd left him, my grandmother and aunt had tried to commit my mother to a mental institution. They took my father's side in the separation. They didn't care what he'd done. A man's behaviour, no matter how bad, my grandmother once told my mother, was just one of the crosses a wife had to bear. After the scandal of that divorce, my mother was drawn to my stepfather on account of his strength, which turned out to be a certain brutishness with which she was all too familiar.

⁂

My mother would never have gone to Australia by herself. She needed someone she could convince to come with her, as if that was the only way she could convince herself. The question for me was why she didn't stay there. For a long time I didn't understand our return to Holland – why she should even *miss* it, after all she'd been through there, after how her family had treated her. I imagined at first that she'd been drawn back to Holland *despite* her family, but I came to realise that it was more complicated than that. The two were one and the same for her. Bergen Op Zoom *was* her family. She was both attracted to and repulsed by her mother and her brothers and sisters. They had a hold over her. It was like a destructive addiction.

And the same dynamic was reflected in her relationships with men. She had never loved my stepfather, not even from the beginning. My older brother and I – though we'd known him from early childhood – had never loved him either, or called him our father. Although he renovated many of the houses we lived in, although he provided a different sort of architecture for the life of our family, there was a sense in which he did not belong with us at all. On some instinctive level, we saw him in the same way that our mother did. But it was this violent, lonely man who travelled with us from place to place, and who, on Bribie Island, painted his arm with black shoe polish and pretended to be a Moor from Spain, so that my brother and I could imagine that Holland was close.

I can picture us all sitting around that tree on Bribie Island, singing, waiting to see if Swarte Piet might knock on our door, not realising that he is with us already. We sing and sing and then my stepfather shifts in his seat, clears his throat, and says that he has to go out for tobacco. While he is out, we keep on singing until suddenly, with a sound like a clap of thunder, the Moor's fist shakes open the door, there is a flash of a black hand, and my brother and I jump in our skins and scramble on the floor for the sweets that come flying in from the darkness.

Arriving home with his tobacco, our stepfather is sorry to have missed all of that, and my brother and I can't believe his bad luck, the terrible timing of it. We show him our hands full of sweets; he pretends to be impressed.

And so, even on the other side of the world, even as their relationship began to collapse, my mother and stepfather maintained this tradition, which enabled them to find a fleeting common ground. It was also a way of declaring allegiance to a place they believed to be somehow better. It was easier to focus on that sense of a better place somewhere else than to focus on what was happening between them. It didn't matter where we were; there was always a way of looking back with that sort of longing. When we were in Australia, they focused on what they called the traditions and cultural depth of Holland; when we returned to Holland, they focused on the open space and opportunities and potential for reinvention in Australia.

Swarte Piet lumbers through my imagination as the symbol of all that; as the symbol of a kind of uneasy relationship to the past: the past that becomes embodied in a place that is simultaneously left behind and *not* left behind, a place that provides an emotional escape hatch, that remains in the consciousness exerting a magnetic pull. It's what the past becomes when you don't look at it directly, when you respond to it without seeing it clearly. The reaction becomes a kind of naive trap, a knee-jerk thing, a wild, hungry scrabbling on the floor. That's why I don't miss Holland anymore, or maintain the traditions my mother brought from it. That's why I have never gone back by myself.

I don't know whether it was my mother who convinced my stepfather to be Swarte Piet on that night in Bribie Island, or whether he came up with the idea himself. But for my entire childhood, I imagined that it had been Swarte Piet himself who had come across to the other side of the world to knock miraculously on our door. I don't know if it was my longing for the sweets, or fear, that kept me from looking beyond that blackened hand, from running through the doorway to stare into the real face on the other side.

MEG MUNDELL
Confessions of a Ditch-Jumper

I came to Australia by boat, vomiting most of the way. It took nine days to cross The Ditch, as the blue bit between Australia and New Zealand is known. The Tasman Sea is a two million square-kilometre expanse of alien territory, as beautiful as it is treacherous. One second you're flying up the peak of a gigantic swell, the next you've dropped into a deep pit, walls of water blocking out the sky. Occasionally a lonely container ship ploughs into view, or a lost bucket floats past. That surreal crossing confirmed the fragility of human life: one slip and you're gone.

When I first reached Australia, I greeted my new homeland by vomiting into one of its beautiful seaports, the aptly named Coffs Harbour. Despite this rudeness, I got a warm welcome: the immigration officers joked as they stamped our passports, asked if we saw many 'fush' on the way over, teased me for lacking sea legs, and threatened to impound our chickpeas on the official grounds that 'they taste like sheet!' (Or 'shut', as we Kiwis call it.)

After docking, we coast-hopped up to Bundaberg. When I spotted a turtle I nearly imploded with excitement; awestruck by my first kangaroo, I crawled towards it David Attenborough-style, making the locals point and laugh. Australia's inventive slang and mysterious history, the tropical heat and fields of sugarcane, the graceful Queenslanders perched on stilts, the tacky neon of Surfers Paradise, the perma-tanned Gold Coast grannies in hotpants and gold bling – all this filled me with wonder. The place was nothing like New Zealand. It felt deeply and thrillingly foreign.

This sense of estrangement wasn't mutual. Australia absorbed me without effort, like dry sand soaks up a drop of water. 'She'll be right, mate,' said the locals. And indeed she was – for me, anyway.

Few boat arrivals get such a friendly welcome in Australia. The term 'boat people', a crude, catch-all phrase for asylum seekers arriving here by sea, lumps together a small group of humans with hugely diverse ethnic backgrounds: South-East Asian, Middle Eastern, African. In the sixteen-odd years since I arrived, I've heard them called many other ugly names: opportunists, parasites, queue-jumpers, scabs. The glaring difference between their reception and mine has always puzzled me. Unlike the (mostly non-white) migrants who risk their lives in crappy boats to seek asylum here, I wasn't fleeing war and persecution: I was doing it for kicks, a free adventure in exchange for crewing duties. Our captain was a sleazebag, but he got us here safely. My seasickness was vile, but our vessel was seaworthy, a yuppie yacht. Nobody drowned or got locked in a detention centre.

I've copped no flack for being a Ditch-Jumper: Australia welcomed me with open arms. No one's ever accused me of stealing their job, jumping a queue, skimping on deodorant or driving taxis in a geographically ill-informed manner. Thanks to a convenient bunch of political, historical and economic ties, Australians and New Zealanders can cross each other's borders without fuss and live and work in either country indefinitely. Australia has gradually restricted Kiwis' access to perks like citizenship, education and social security, but it's still relatively easy for us to set up nest here. Drawn by bigger cities and better work prospects, we migrate to Australia in droves – roughly 30,000 Kiwis hop the Ditch annually, and half a million New Zealand citizens currently live here – yet the tabloids and shock jocks don't describe us as a 'flood'. And unlike African, Arabic or Asian immigrants, no one tells me to 'integrate'; they assume, quite wrongly, that I've already done so.

But I don't feel integrated. When people talk about 'Australian values', an oft-used phrase here, I genuinely don't know what they're on about. I don't get 'mateship': to me it sounds like the password to an ageing boys' club. I'm fond of donkeys, but Simpson's celebrated specimen doesn't symbolise anything to me. Nor do I barrack for a footy team – or even care about footy. (When I confessed this to a group of new workmates, an awkward silence gave way to expressions of dismay, pity and outright suspicion. One guy wanted to revoke my Australian citizenship; maybe he was joking, but he sounded truly offended.) And the term 'un-Australian' bugs me no end. What the hell does it mean? Since I don't know, it probably applies to me.

Yet somehow, Kiwis escape the xenophobia and hostility directed at many non-white immigrants. We also sidestep the specific ribbing aimed at people from the United Kingdom (Australia's 'Mother Country') and the United States (its political big brother), the two nations wielding the greatest cultural influence here: the casual references to 'whingeing Poms', the open jibes aimed at Americans.

Yes, racism exists in every nation, including New Zealand. But what strikes me about anti-migrant sentiments here in Australia is that they're often voiced to me quite openly, as if I obviously share these views. I've had numerous conversations in which locals slag off immigrants, forgetting that I'm a blow-in myself – and unless they're Aboriginal, they too come from migrant stock. I've heard it in outback roadhouses, on short-lived dates, even among a supposedly leftie group of chardonnay-quaffing pals.

I still regret my cowardice in letting some of these comments slide. Years ago, I was on a first date with a young Aussie guy in a Thai restaurant, and a group of international students passed our table. Gob full of pad thai, he let rip about 'bloody Asians, walking around jabbering in their own language'. Shocked, I responded primly that Aboriginal people could justifiably say the same about us whiteys, then snuck off to the loo to activate the emergency 'phone-a-friend' escape tactic (housemate locked out, sorry to rush off, etc.). I dumped his racist arse the next day, making no bones about why, but wish I'd been more vocal at the time. Now, when someone drops a casual remark about 'queue-jumpers' or 'bloody immigrants', I bluntly point out that they're talking to a bloody immigrant. What makes me so different?

It seems the price of not copping that animosity has been an erasure of my own claim to difference. I've lost count of the times I've heard: 'But Kiwis are just like us! You're practically Australian!' It's meant as a compliment, but I hate hearing this. I don't feel Australian, and probably never will, despite the dual citizenship I was granted with surprising ease. National identity can't be forced on a person; it just doesn't work that way. Besides, Kiwis are different from Australians: we even pronounce 'different' differently.

When Australian commentators discuss the 'migrant experience', or the country's 'multicultural richness', Kiwis are often conspicuously absent from these accounts. Here, the public face of Kiwiness exists only at a surface level: in the jokey quibbles over Phar Lap's citizenship (New Zealand born and bred – can we have his heart back, please?), who invented pavlova (we did) and the origins of Vegemite (Australian). In the good-natured teasing about our accent ('Say "seeex"!') and the persistent sheep jokes – at which we roll our eyes, knowing them for the dark glimpse into the Australian psyche that they so clearly are. In brief nods to *The Lord of the Rings*, the All Blacks and bungee jumping.

Beyond that, Australians show a benign, entrenched and profound disinterest in New Zealand culture; indeed, that very phrase is assumed to be an oxymoron. Like a friendly but slightly patronising older cousin, Australia welcomes us in, but shows little curiosity about our heritage, our history or our *tangata whenua* (Indigenous peoples: literally, 'people of the land'). While other 'Other' cultures spark a range of reactions – from admiration to envy, wariness to outright hostility – New Zealanders are expected to just melt into the background, perhaps an unspoken tax for our border-hopping privileges. Hell, you never see Melbourne's Federation Square hired out for a Kiwi-themed cultural festival. Stink, bro (not good, mate)!

Given the sheer numbers of New Zealand expats living here, this is puzzling. It's also annoying and insulting: nobody likes having their identity overlooked, their roots ignored, their homeland dismissed as inconsequential. Kiwis are supposedly a reserved lot, but this cultural blind spot is enough to make us pack a sad (sulk): 'For Chrissakes guys, give us some credit for being foreign!'

We've got the ferocious *haka* (war dance), interactive *ti rakau* (stick-tossing games) and hypnotic *poi* (dance with tethered balls swung in rhythmic patterns); delicious *hangi* (earth oven) food and feijoa jam; unique carving and weaving traditions; decent homegrown hip-hop, and the *Flight of the Conchords* boys. All totally choice (excellent), bro. Dammit Australia, we want our community festival – and we want it now. Rattle your dags (hurry up)!

The differences between New Zealand and Australia go way beyond the semantic quirks of chilly bins (eskie), jandals (thongs) and judder bars (speed humps). Take geography. Kiwis are the spawn of a mountainous landscape: what Aussies refer to as a 'hill', we classify as a gentle slope. This causes us problems when following directions over here: many's the time I've searched in vain for a landmark 'hill', only to discover that I've apparently been going 'up' and 'down' the thing for hours (the so-called Paris End of Collins Street, Melbourne, is just one example).

Pesky seagulls might steal our chups, but Kiwis find their squawking presence reassuring, proof that the coast is nearby. By contrast, Australia's vast inland deserts make us nervous; in our skinny zigzag of a country, you're never more than 90 minutes' drive from the sea. The surrounding ocean gives New Zealand a distinctive clarity to its light: even on overcast days, returning expats notice it as soon as they step off the plane. We also grew up in a land of earthquake drills: basically, when our primary-school teacher yelled out 'Earthquake!' in the middle of maths, we hid under our desks. (Despite the fact that my grandmother narrowly survived the 1931 Napier earthquake, which razed her home city and killed 256 people, the reality of our unstable landscape didn't hit home for me until the horror of the recent Christchurch quakes.)

Then there's language. New Zealand has two official names: the original is Aotearoa, 'land of the long white cloud', bestowed by the Māori people's ancestors when they first spotted the place from their canoes around 600 years ago. While Australia originally had around 250 distinct Indigenous languages, plus numerous dialects, comparatively tiny Aotearoa has just one. This has probably helped the renaissance of Māori culture: presumably it's easier for native peoples to present a unified front when they share one language. It's also meant that most *pakeha* (whitefellas) have a basic grasp of Māori via the simple words we all learned at primary school – *kia ora* (hi or be well), *kai* (food), *aroha* (love, compassion), *ka pai* (good), *wahine* (woman), *whānau* (extended family), *whare* (home), *puku* (belly), *pakaru* (broken), *mana* (respect, authority), *e hoa* (friend), *kia kaha* (be strong or my thoughts are with you). Many *pakeha*, myself included, feel a vicarious pride in Māori culture; it's not cultural appropriation, but a quiet affinity that's woven into us early and deep, at the level of childhood memory, old songs and daily conversation.

All Kiwi passports are printed in both English and Māori. When my German-born boyfriend asked me to translate the Māori sections, I had to admit I'd lost my schoolgirl grasp of it. Back home, you hear Māori spoken every day – in chit-chat and place names, on bilingual TV and radio – but without this regular exposure, I've sadly lost my ear for its tones and patterns. Yet *te reo* Māori is a beautiful language, at once lyrical and practical, poetic and phonetic: *Tena! Kei roto I tēnei uruwhenua tētahi taonga tahiko.* ('Attention! This passport contains a contactless integrated circuit chip which is an electronic device.')

Spoken aloud, Māori turns even bureaucratic waffle into lyrical music. My meagre classroom remnants don't get much use these days; I practice on my cat – *Tena koe, kaiako!* (Hello, teacher!) – but he's nth-generation Aussie, so the poetry is lost on him.

Sixteen years on, despite the dual citizenship, I still travel on my Kiwi passport, and have resisted getting an Australian one. I love both places, but in very different ways; I've made a good life here in Oz, but I'm still profoundly homesick. I miss my parents, and my homeland, too – the smell of baking *kumara* (native sweet potato), the calls of Mopoke owls, the ridiculously steep hills and cute, clipped vowels. I miss a land of crashing surf, boiling mud, quaint dairies (milk bars) and dodgy TV, where you can take a weekend tiki tour (casual drive or road trip), driving the length of the country with a ferry trip in between; where tall plumes of *toe toe* grass wave like blonde flames by the roadside, and you can buy *hangi* food from highway caravans. A place peppered with *Marae* (traditional meeting houses) and rich in Polynesian culture; the first country in the world where women won the vote, back in 1893. A place so spatially isolated that it doesn't bother trying to mimic Europe or America.

Nostalgia is a lovely thing, but migrants must also face the realities of the homelands we've left. Right now, despite its pluses – and there are many – New Zealand has a conservative (read: centre-right) government, a millionaire prime minister, an unappealing wage gap, dwindling state assets and the world's biggest case of brain drain. Like all small places, it's also subject to the limits of scale. Kiwis are a pragmatic lot, and Australia offers a greater range of career opportunities. I confess, that's what brought me here — that, and the lure of an adventure at sea.

My boat trip sparked an odd mix of emotions: elation and fear, novelty and nausea; an uneasy sense of being cast adrift, lost between places, neither here nor there. This weird tangle of feelings still lingers — not as the remnants of seasickness, but as part of a syndrome that I suspect is common to migrants everywhere. Starting over in a new place is exciting. But sometimes you feel homesick and disorientated, all at sea, like you don't belong anywhere. Uprooted and plonked down in unfamiliar surrounds, you lose your personal reference points, the things that tell you who you are. You find yourself up late, typing the word 'Kiwiana' into Google; hankering for a bowl of hokey pokey (honeycomb) ice-cream; you call home, and they express concern about your fading accent.

Migration always has a cost, and I know I've gotten off comparatively lightly (what's a little erasure between friends?). But my real fear is that New Zealand has, in return, forgotten me. You turn your back on a place for too long, and it can happen. I want to go home more often — to see my folks, reconnect with the place, straighten out my vowels. But as the years pass, it's disconcerting to witness how little you are missed. I recently emailed a New Zealand academic, introducing myself as a Kiwi author living abroad, and was horrified when she wrote back describing me as someone who 'used to be a New Zealander'. Ouch: my Kiwi identity erased, with just sux luttle words. When did this vanishing act begin? Is it reversible?

In 2001, when I'd been living here for six years, then Prime Minister John Howard's churlish reprimand to 'boat people' rang in my ears: '*We* will decide who comes to this country, and the circumstances in which they come.' What a total egg (idiot)! This statement always struck me as the petulant shout of a schoolyard bully, lording it over the communal sandpit. But its resonance lingers. Too often, immigrants who criticise Australia's immigration policies get this response: 'If you don't like it, go back where you came from!' Don't rock the boat; be thankful, or be silent.

Well, stuff that. In my heart I still don't feel Australian, but I do feel that I'm part of the Australian community. I'm also a signed-up citizen, with all the attendant rights and responsibilities – and to me, that includes questioning some of the weird contradictions in how we treat 'other' cultures, and asking why Aussies won't give our *poi* at least a cursory whirl. By some strange collision of luck and circumstance, Australia chose to let me into its sandpit. I'll try not to vomit into it, but I refuse to disappear.

PAOLA TOTARO

Pointing North

The sensation remains vivid: palpitating heart and shaking, sweaty hands. It happened every day without fail, at roll call during my last year of primary school. Checked in alphabetical order, I'd be holding my breath by the time the name before mine was called out. The teacher – I still remember his name and face – was also the school's deputy principal, and for some inexplicable reason revelled in calling me 'Potato Tomato' instead of Paola Totaro. Perhaps it was hard to pronounce, perhaps he just thought it was a bit of fun, but the truth is that the guffaw of laughter from the other kids, regular as clockwork, was a daily ordeal.

School life as an Italian kid in an Anglo, well-to-do Sydney neighbourhood in the early 1970s was a jarring mix of joy and trepidation. We lived in a quiet cul-de-sac, had the run of an enormous nature reserve at the end of the street, the freshest of air, a swimming pool and the kind of space to roam and play that you'd only dream of in urban Italy. My next-door-neighbour and best friend and I built cubby houses, talked across the fence, rode our bikes for hours and would disappear, free as birds, coming home only for a feed or to sleep.

Monday to Friday, however, often dawned with a deep sense of dread. Etched deeply is the memory of the very last day of primary school, when a frenetic game of chasing in the playground ended with a crash onto the asphalt and my left arm. It was painful and yes, I sobbed. The same teacher decided my tears were those of a 'hysterical Italian', forcing me to wait until the school bell sounded at 3pm, when my mother came to pick me up. An X-ray taken that afternoon showed a fracture and I spent that summer with my arm in plaster.

High school wasn't too much fun, either. There, it was a group of boys, not the teachers, who dealt it out. They too figured my name was too hard to pronounce, so 'Greasy Wog' became my moniker. In Year 7, I was assigned to share a desk with the ringleader. I remember his name and face too, but also his hair, his sweaty teenage-boy smell and the way he'd hiss quietly, 'You've got a pig's arse, you wog', as if it were yesterday.

That dissonance between a newcomer's sense of themselves and the outside world's perception fascinated me as a young adult, and later as a journalist. I found myself intrigued by what made people tick, by the life experiences that led individuals, whether they be politicians, ordinary citizens or criminals, to act as they do. I am convinced that always feeling on the periphery – not being 'one of them' but not 'one of us' either – made me observe and report news through a slightly different prism, one where I had a natural bent for the outsider, and perhaps a hypersensitivity to injustice.

The funny thing is that none of this childhood teasing really meant that much at the time. It hurt, was occasionally scary, but in the end, that's just the way things were. For some years, I even wondered if I'd imagined it. A visit from a school friend I hadn't seen in nearly forty years put paid to that this year. She not only remembered it clearly, but brought a lump to my throat by apologising for other kids whom she'd abhorred anyway. I suspect now that the 'hysterical Italian' label embedded itself deeply into my psyche, forcing a kind of internal sweeping under the carpet to avoid accusations of exaggeration. Downplaying it all probably also helped survive it.

Still, I adored Australia – riding my bike in streets with no traffic, having dogs and cats, adopting wounded birds and keeping a turtle. We spent half our lives swimming, revelling in sunshine and joyous liberty. I had no real sense of what day-to-day life might have been like in Italy had we not left, as I was not quite four years old when we moved to Australia. But in my psyche, extended family – grandparents, cousins, uncles and aunts – symbolised 'home' and this was reinforced by the regular trips back, courtesy of Dad's job. For a sun-lover the timing of these returns was perfect: usually mid-winter in Australia and mid-summer in the northern hemisphere. Life was an endless summer.

In many ways, it was an idyllic existence, and yet my 'otherness' just wouldn't go away. For years, I'd mumble

– ashamed – 'I'm Italian' when asked the provenance of my name. I don't know how many times people said 'You're Italian? Our grocer/vegie man/deli lady's Italian and you don't look/sound Italian.'

As if that was a compliment.

Dad, tongue stuck firmly in cheek, decided on a couple of occasions that if people *expected* us to be fruit-and-vegie sellers, then he'd help fulfil the prejudice. My father is as much a gardener as I am an astrophysicist, but he gleefully pretended to stake out a vegetable garden in our perfectly manicured, middle-class front lawn. He took the joke one rather large step further one day by bringing home a pet goat. I've no idea where he got the animal. We named her Olga and Dad triumphantly joked that if Australians expected Italian goatherds, he'd indulge that expectation, too. Olga was with us just a few weeks until my mother, well and truly over the goat poo around the pool, despatched our four-legged friend to a Catholic monastery in Sydney's rural west. (Or so we were told: a barbecue was Olga's rather more likely fate.)

I don't remember any other non-Aussie kids at school: no Greeks, no Asian kids who might share the experience. I wonder if there had been, what I would have done? Would I have found a group to fit into? Would that sense of being the outsider have been shared? All my friends were Australian and the only Italians I knew of my age were the weekend friendships forged with the children of other expats. The difference was that they went back home after a couple of years, while we never did.

As time went on, my parents embraced Australia definitively: Dad dumped Fiat, the executive job that had brought him to Australia, and went on to found the nation's first Ethnic Affairs Commission for the NSW Government. Mum finished her law degree long-distance but switched disciplines, forging a distinguished university career teaching Italian and applied linguistics. My parents both took Australian citizenship; my brother, who is now an intensive-care specialist, was born in Melbourne. None of them have ever doubted their choices.

And yet I resisted, refusing stubbornly to take citizenship in Australia because, at the time, Italy wouldn't allow dual nationality. Today I could have two passports but I've chosen not to.

Why? I honestly don't know.

In adolescence, this love affair with Italy conflicted rather eccentrically with a secret aspiration to temper and anglicise my innately Latin character. Every Monday, in an earnest morning ritual in front of the bathroom mirror, I'd resolve that I'd be 'as cool as a cucumber', acting in what I perceived to be the Anglo way. I failed miserably, without fail. Our neighbours (parents of my best friend, Lindy) were probably my role models: they seemed to always speak in hushed tones, lived by what appeared to be clockwork routine and never displayed emotion of any sort in public, unlike our volcanic household.

I remember these *feelings* much more than events as I grew. I had the sensation of being loud – we Italians shout; it's a cultural thing, I guess – and this was always accompanied by a heightened impression of being uncomfortably *visible*. The word *basta* – 'stop, enough!' – was heard often from our parents, particularly when we were making too much noise outside, but it would be years before we realised with great laughter that our neighbours had thought that our parents were calling us 'bastards'!

I was also naturally outspoken and talked way too much in class; perhaps I was overly boisterous. Overwhelmingly, my desire was to melt in; not to disappear but just to feel…well, less obvious. Anglicising my name to Paula irritated me at the most fundamental level but it was also a blessed relief. Even more wonderful was an instinctive decision, on my first *Sydney Morning Herald* byline in 1981, to reclaim Paola once and for all. To this day, particularly in the age of Facebook, long-lost friendships and unexpected hook-ups, I am reminded of my two lives: Paula versus Paola, the former an insecure schoolgirl harbouring a fierce love of where she came from but mortified by the lens Australia had applied to her origins; the latter boosted by finding a voice while writing in Australia as the nation began to embrace the cultural, linguistic and epicurean patrimony brought by the wave of post-war migrants.

Memory is a strange and unreliable thing, shaped often by a vignette, captured in a scent, a sound, a shard of emotion rather than factual detail. I've no real recollection of our leaving Italy, for example. It must have been a seminal moment, that emotional farewell from beloved grandparents – Mum was the youngest, Dad an only child – but I see only the photograph of me taken the night before: a single, black-and-white snapshot of a dark, tousle-haired child, sleeping with her arms around a much-loved and worn toy dog. I was oblivious to the enormity of what was unfolding around my family.

As soon as I started working, first in a small media company, then as a *Herald* cadet, every saved cent went towards an airline ticket to return to Italy to see my grandparents and get a dose of Naples, my birthplace. These visits felt like a drug, a recharging of my existential batteries, a plugging in to something that felt 'right', even if it lasted for only a short time. I remember lying in the sun on my grandparents' terrace overlooking the bay and Vesuvius and reading David Malouf's *Johnno* when I was twenty years old. Schlepping Australian novels with me to Italy became a private ritual, and never have I felt as happy as when mired in the gentle sea and sunshine beside the Mediterranean while breathing in the literature of the island continent where I grew up, a place I knew intimately but, somehow, preferred from afar.

I married in Australia, became the mother of two girls and stepmum to two boys – all of them patriotic Aussies – and work for Australian newspapers in a profession I am, luckily, hard-wired to love more every day. Australia provided me with the myriad opportunities that only a civilised, democratic meritocracy is able to offer to the child of migrant expatriates. I am happy, and feel incredibly fortunate in every way, to have grown up in Australia. But I never felt quite at home – or 'myself' – in Australia. I still don't.

This *could* have made me a malcontent, a whinger pining constantly for a world I'd never actually 'lived' in. Instead, it fostered a desire to compare constantly; to listen and be open to the stories of others; to see different possibilities, experiences and ways of looking at the society I lived and grew up in; to experiment and be adventurous. Professor Martin Krygier, in his Boyer lecture *Beyond Fear and Hope*, calls people like himself and me cultural 'hybrids'. He argues that this hybrid space can provide a unique vantage point, even if it often feels like a peculiar place to stand.

'That metaphorical space is simultaneously inside and outside the cultures in which they were raised, in which they live, of which they are parts and which are part of them,' he wrote. 'More generally, it can offer a powerful antidote to parochialism, which has, perhaps, cosy charms *as* a way of life, but is not much help in understanding or evaluating a way of life.' Oh, how I understand that! I *feel* it, and indeed live it. If you're not part of something, it's natural to look outside to see where you might fit in. And if you don't, the instinct is to search and wonder what it is about the culture you live in that's unable to look beyond itself.

That constant comparison, omnipresent in people like us, can make you hypercritical of your adoptive home, or else can help identify and provide a powerful, fresh appreciation that 'native' Aussie colleagues and 'non-hybrid' friends take for granted or find unremarkable. Krygier's observations were a bolt of lightning for me. As a journalist, particularly during many years writing domestic politics, I was inclined to compare policy decisions with those of other countries, not other Australian cities or states. When the issue of heroin injecting rooms was being debated in Sydney, there was near universal scepticism that it would ever get through the parliament.

In my mind I thought, Europe had done it years before, so why shouldn't we?

Now, decades on – and living and working in England, of all places – I've started to understand how powerful growing up in Australia has been for me, and that perhaps it is being neither Italian nor Australian that has truly shaped who I am.

I've confronted some painful fantasies: that longing of old, the sense of 'home', the Italy of my childhood –

constructs of great sentiment, but of imagination more than reality. Like the old-timers, the wave of post-war immigrants that wrought Australians' perceptions of Italians in my childhood, my vision of Italy had remained idealistic, trapped in another time.

Italy has changed. I still move regularly between London and Naples; I love it, Napoli, but I couldn't live there if you paid me. I now see Italy through Australian eyes, and have become anglicised in ways I never could have expected. I am intolerant of the Italian disdain for the urban environment, and the inability to value, care for and maintain its enormous cultural patrimony. I despair at the inefficiency and corruption of the political system, the nepotism that flavours the labour market and the cultural emphasis on *la bella figura*, which values grooming, being well turned out and living in a well-kept home over national pride and a collective respect for the public domain.

England is anathema to this and probably why I feel so utterly at ease here. Yet unlike the English (and Italians), I am imbued with an Australian contempt for divisions of class, for overt shows of elitism and blatant nepotism. I have a great love of humour that prickles the pompous, but also understand – and have argued publicly and in print – the significance of a living monarchy in a democratic society like Britain's. I'd hope that my default intellectual and political position is flexible, untrammelled by old-world prejudice, and non-judgemental when it comes to sex, race and class.

That is Australian, I think – and a gift of growing up there with 'hybrid' parents who shared and embraced those values.

My life is seasoned by this theme of 'otherness', peppered with longing and internal confusion. It is as if when we left Italy, my internal compass – but not that of my parents – simply couldn't stop pointing north.

Now, I choose to live in Europe. The truth is, I feel absolutely right here. But the prism through which I see the world has no limits and no borders. It was Australia that showed me this new way.

CHI VU

The Uncanny

I

One task of a migrant is to move from a sense of alienation in the new country to a sense of being comfortable with that alienation. One of the tasks of a writer is to move between thinking about content and form, in order to heighten the 'what' of the story by selecting the best genre for the piece. An author who writes about migration faces the twin tasks of addressing alienation and form.

Imagine you are a migrant who had been a member of the primary ethnic, cultural and linguistic group in your old country. Then, after migrating, you are suddenly part of a minority in a new country. There is no shared cultural context between you and the majority of the people around you. Perhaps the only thing that most people know about where you came from is the name of a distant war. Little else outside of that frame is understood by the people in your street, at your school or workplace. As though overnight, you find yourself viewed through a small frame not of your choosing. This limited view amputates you: it narrows how you are understood, and therefore what you can communicate.

And vice versa.

II

My family arrived in our new country in the middle of winter, 1979. In the morning, steam came out of our mouths and there was dew on the grass. We spent the first days settling into the migrant hostel in Maribyrnong, in the western suburbs of Melbourne. All food was served at the canteen, as cooking was not allowed in our living quarters. Breakfast was cereal and milk, and lunch consisted of pre-packed sandwiches, which I quickly got used to. But dinner was always a big adjustment: you would collect your own plastic tray, put a plate on it and get served a large hunk of meat flavoured with salt and pepper – no other flavours. The vegetables had been boiled and came without any dipping sauces. No matter how much salt you added, the food did not become more flavoursome; it merely became saltier.

After a few days we ventured out of the hostel to explore this new world. We were waiting for a bus when we saw a sign that read: NO STANDING ANY TIME. My father must have read it several times, perplexed, before he called my oldest sister over. She was considered the authority as she had actually applied herself to learn English from the private tutor while we were still in Vietnam, while the rest of us kids had only followed her around making foreign-sounding, silly noises at each other. My sixteen-year-old sister stepped forward and read it carefully. Then she turned around and confirmed: 'Yes, it's true – it says we are not allowed to stand here – at any time.' My father's mouth turned grim and his whole bearing seemed to drop, for perhaps we'd made a terrible mistake. Could it be that we had risked our lives on the open seas to arrive at an even more repressive regime than the one we had just escaped from? The bus stop was right here, and yet we were not permitted to stand. In this impossible predicament, we each then tried to find some pose that could be interpreted, if it came down to an unfair prosecution, that was not in fact standing: slouching, leaning against the pole, poised about to dash away; I think one or two of us children may have even squatted by the side of the road, Vietnamese-style.

Before the end of the day, we realised that everyone ignored these signs, and in fact stood shamelessly, blatantly, next to or in front of the NO STANDING ANY TIME sign. I made a mental note: the word 'standing' had been used in a peculiar way and only applied to cars, which could neither stand nor sit nor squat.

As we settled in, we needed to find a way to taste our own food again. One of my parents, probably my mother, took things in her own hands and discovered a Chinese grocery somewhere in the city. She came home with provisions: jars of fermented pastes and sauces that warmed our nostrils. We bought a little electric cooker and began cooking food in our living quarters in the migrant hostel. I vaguely recall the boiling of vermicelli and the scent of a hot pot emanating from the electric cooker. Perhaps someone kept a lookout at the slightly open window for anyone official who might have been walking the grounds that evening, and to fan the plumes of pungent steam out the window.

We ate this delicious, welcoming food. It was like our innards unclenched and smiled for the first time in this new country. We were able to relax and take in our situation better. My mother and sisters started cleaning up, putting away our contraband cooking utensils. There was some stock spilt on the floor, which I slipped on as I went past. I fell, and hit my head on the pointy corner of the wall.

The next day at the migrant hostel school (a learning centre to help us adjust) the female teacher was yelling at me, but I didn't want to answer her. She wanted to know what had happened, why did I have this big cut on my head, why was there dried blood sticking down my black hair where this lump had formed. I started to stammer and quiver. I told her in my best English, calling on all my efforts to make some sense.

'My mother cooking…water on the ground, I falling.' Then I would have brought my hands up to my wound to indicate the impact with the pointy corner of the wall. The teacher's anger seemed to subside and she left me alone. I remained mortified at what I had revealed under pressure. I had also used the word 'ground' instead of 'floor', so now she probably thought we lived in a mud hut in Vietnam.

At my earliest chance, I ran back to our hostel and told my father what had happened: how the teacher screamed at me about the cut on my head; how I told her that we had been cooking illegally in our rooms.

'We're going to be in so much trouble, aren't we?'

I started to think that they would send my family away to whatever this country's equivalent of the New Economic Zone was – to scratch out a life in dense virgin jungle, to die from dirty water, malnutrition and mosquito bites. I started to plan how we'd have to pack all our belongings, again, before they came to get us. Unbelievably, my father was smiling gently and looking above me, as though he was imagining the teacher who had shown this concern. 'It's okay,' he reassured, 'you didn't say anything wrong. It's okay, my daughter.'

III

From the time I knew any language at all, I had dreamt and thought and spoken in Vietnamese. The music of it was like rain dropping on tropical leaves growing at different angles, making variously pitched staccatos and then tinkling down into rivulets. My first contact with English was exposure to the strange resonances it made inside my mouth; the adding of 's' on the end of everything, so it seemed at the time; the collapsing of all social relationships into the single pronoun 'you' and its mirror 'I'.

Before we knew enough English to understand everything we were hearing, we learnt the shape of the words from television jingles – singing them loudly, with each of the words made up of similar-sounding Vietnamese words. The word *xe đap* (bicycle) was close enough to 'shut up' for us kids to use. Words like this became a tool of subversion, for if we were caught saying it, we would look nonchalant and say, 'What? Bicycle…'

Less than a year after my family's arrival in Australia, I experienced that moment of unconsciously thinking in the adopted language. I was standing on the wooden steps in my public primary school when this foreign thought arrived. The mind – *my* mind – had thought directly in English without my willing it, without having put any effort into creating it. I stood there frozen on the wooden steps, wanting to burn that moment into my memory, for it was as surprising as suddenly growing a third arm and watching it wave back at me for the first time.

I was part of a wave of immigration fortunate enough not to have to amputate my 'birth' limbs, as my host country took on a more pluralistic stance by the mid 1970s. Those limbs remain under my jacket, weak and pale, yet ageing with the rest of me. I take them out now and again to grasp the texture of words and ideas, to finger-tap quiet rhythms with those tiny fingernails, to listen for the resonances within. They can also be useful when I need to reconnect with a time when my actions did not necessarily represent those of my entire race; they were just mine and my interlocutor's to answer for. My 'alien' limbs are now strong through daily use, so that I can no longer imagine myself without them. After more than thirty years in Australia, my dominant language has become English. It shapes my conscious thoughts, while the Vietnamese still shapes my feelings. So how does this affect my approach to writing?

Given the double blow of cultural and linguistic displacement (both the 'content' and 'form' of one's life becomes unfamiliar as a result of migration), it then follows that the self is also experienced as uncanny. Who is the 'I' in this exchange speaking this encountered language? How is one to approach the 'I' to draw out its many-faceted secrets? How can this 'I' be both familiar yet estranged from an original and undivided 'I' (if such a person ever existed)?

I don't mean to be slippery or sly with my different aliases and identities; I cannot write about a self, using a single 'I', when this self is fragmented.

IV

When I was in grade three, my parents were able to send me to a nearby Catholic school. They had the impression from the French colonial period in Vietnam that Catholic schools offered greater opportunities and provided a more formal and therefore stricter education. They were not to know that the Irish Catholics had been an oppressed minority in Australia's early settlement, and perhaps held more firmly to their beliefs as a result.

It was at my new school that I was introduced to the idea of an all-powerful, omniscient God. Until then I had been without this knowledge, but now that I had it I felt my world changing. During recess I went to the loo, and still heard the strident voice warning us: *God watches us always. Always.* I had a moment that could be considered a parallel with Adam and Eve's after they had eaten from the fruit of knowledge, where they suddenly realised their nakedness, became ashamed and hid from God. Except I was thinking, why would a powerful God watch a little kid in the toilet? Why? I couldn't understand the teaching I'd been given. Rather than feeling shame, I felt a vague sense of dismay.

My teachers were caring and attentive. I learnt to say the Lord's Prayer. I settled in with a group of Vietnamese girls, and we played a high-jump game called 'elastics' – all day, every day – using rubber bands that we'd hand-braided together into a thick cord. I was happy.

Living in a new country is a series of conscious and unconscious decisions about what you hold onto and what you let go of. Many are superficial choices, or are minor in their consequences. Some have long-lasting effects on how others view you, on which doors will be opened or closed to you – and which doors you will try to keep open, despite the price.

In grade four, the children in my class were to go through First Communion. My homeroom teacher asked me whether I wanted to take part in this ceremony as well, and I guess if I had truly wanted to do it, my parents would have supported me. After all, I was the one who had introduced the idea of Santa Claus and the Tooth Fairy to them, and they went along with it.

In religion class, we had started learning about the woman who had spent her whole life in pleasure, wearing perfume and make-up, never lifting a hand to help the poor, being carried up some mountain by her slaves. But then she became sick and was going to die, even though she was still young and beautiful. Just before she died, she renounced her sinful lifestyle, and accepted Jesus Christ as the saviour. So she was accepted into the kingdom of heaven. A conversation between that teacher and I went like this:

'What? She gets to go to heaven?'

'Yes.'

'Because she said she accepted that Jesus was the Son of God?'

'That's right.'

'And there's no other way to get into heaven?'

'You don't have to wait until you're about to die – you can accept Jesus now…'

'Even if you were, like, Gandhi, you wouldn't be able to go to heaven?'

We must have just learnt about Gandhi in history class.

'Not unless he accepted that Jesus Christ is the Son of God.'

'But he was a man of peace, while that woman spent her life selfishly. She gets to go to heaven, but Gandhi goes to hell?'

'If she accepts Jesus, she can go to heaven.'

I thought about all my uncles, aunties, their children (dispersed across the globe after the war), and my parents and siblings who would all burn in hell. And if I accepted this First Communion, I would go to heaven where it would be nice, but there would be no one I knew. And in talking about heaven, if you were genuinely a saint like Gandhi – who although he was Hindu, was a man of peace – wouldn't you feel so upset that you were in this nice place while all these other people were being tortured in hell? If you were a saint that would upset you, and you would probably give up your place in heaven to save someone else.

I told my homeroom teacher and the assistant principal that I didn't want to undergo First Communion with the other kids. They looked at me, at each other, and then back at me. Something in my teacher's eyes dimmed when she looked at me after that, as though she had done her best to save my soul, but it was ultimately up to me.

The day arrived. My fellow classmates, who had been so nervous before the ceremony, came streaming out of the school church, so proud and confident. The boys looked dapper in their suits, shirts and polished shoes, and the girls beamed with joy in their white dresses and white veils (white being the colour of death in Vietnam when worn on the head). I waited in the shadows with the other kids who did not undergo First Communion as they held even stricter religious beliefs than Christianity, imagining the crackling flames of damnation licking at our feet.

V

The task here is actually to untangle which consequences are due to being a migrant, and which are due to having fled Vietnam as a refugee. The impact of the latter comes down to this: that when things get really difficult, as they do once in a while, I remember that my family and I could have all easily died at sea, no problem, no trace, unable to be found, as was the fate of up to half a million of our contemporaries. Anything from that time onwards is to be considered 'bonus points'.

In writing the above, it seems that some small part of me (and I assume of each member of my family as well) did die on our journey over. For a consciousness of the truth of our deaths is itself a form of death, even though our bodies are safe and sound. For the miracle of land and birdcall and halcyon dawn afterwards is now bled with the passage of time. For when we next face the abyss, we already know its fathomless darkness, its ceaseless horror.

MALLA NUNN

An Unanswered Prayer

Twelve years ago, my aunties, uncles, cousins, nephews and nieces crammed into a small red-brick house in Perth's southern suburbs. It was May, the lawns made green by early rains and overshadowed by wattle trees. My grandmother lay in a back room, attended by a roster of relatives. She was bedridden by then, her body beneath the covers the one still point in the constant flow of activity brought on by her dying. My aunts cooked ox-tail soup and biryani in the kitchen. Some of the men cleaned the homemade barbecue in the backyard and others tinkered with cars in the garage. Children, all first-generation Australians, ran circles in the grass while flocks of black cockatoos flew over the garden, squawking.

All the available space in the house was filled with spare beds, plastic toys and people. The washing machine worked twelve-hour shifts to supply clean sheets and pillowcases for the long-term stay-overs and the overnighters. Every morning a home-care nurse would come to the house to dispense morphine tablets and other medical supplies to my grandmother. Without fail, the nurses commented on the multiple generations and skin colours squeezed into the house and then would ask the inevitable question, 'And where are you all from?'

Fragrant cups of red-bush tea on the lounge-room table, the smell of curry in the kitchen and a TV tuned to *Neighbours* while Miriam Makeba blasted from another room — all screamed 'New Australian.'

'We're from Southern Africa,' whoever was on meds duty would say.

'Where in South Africa?'

Port Elizabeth, Swaziland, Durban, Zululand, Johannesburg, take your pick. But a geographical explanation of our origins rarely satisfied. What the person asking the question really wanted to know was, 'How did you come into being? Who made you?'

We understood their confusion. A blonde toddler lounged on the lap of a teenage girl with dark skin and sloping brown eyes. A group of women with varying degrees of tightness to their curly hair set out trays of biscuits for morning tea. Over in a corner, reading the classified section of the *West Australian* newspaper, sat a man who might be part Indian, or maybe Sicilian.

'We're mixed-race,' one of us would explain. 'A bit of German, Zulu, Dutch, English, Swazi, Scottish and French.'

'Is that so?' the nurses would say. It was interesting, this melting pot of colours in a suburban house, but beyond that they didn't seem to consider us in any way racially tainted. Twenty-five years after my father packed a nervous wife and four children into a Nissan, lashed two steamer trunks to the roof-rack with rope and drove down the wild coast of South Africa to Cape Town to board the ship to Perth, we had fully integrated. We were exotic, yes, but exotic Australians.

Back in Swaziland, mixed-race people (or 'coloured people', as we used to be called) like us were caught between the Black and White worlds, and had to create a smaller world of our own. We did not go unnoticed by the others, however. Traditional Zulus and Swazis said of us, 'You are your *mother's* child' – in a culture where children belonged to the father, we were an aberration, an abnormality. We had no clan. The British and the Dutch blamed each other for our dusky appearance.

'When your father said he was taking you all to Australia,' my grandmother was fond of telling us, 'I begged God to change his mind. Why, I prayed, must he move his family so far from home?'

Later, she would praise God for not listening to her.

It was 1972 when we left. We lived on the grounds of a boarding school set up especially for mixed-race children. My father was the boys' master, my mother an English and history teacher. A slim dirt road with cattle grids at the entry and exit cut past the brick church, the graveyard and then the fruit orchard before easing down a slope to the student dormitories, classrooms and staff houses. A diesel generator powered the lights, which went off each night at nine. Behind the classrooms, the land dropped away to grass fields and craggy mountains. The rarely heard sound of a car engine brought us running from wherever we were to wave and sprint in the dust left by the car's tyres. Even by the standards of a tiny, landlocked British Protectorate, we lived in a backwater.

Ten days after leaving Cape Town, our ship, the Italian-registered *Marconi*, sounded its horn when the Australian coast came into view. Tugboats churned the water and gulls flew across the bow. Italians, Greeks, Croatians and South Africans crowded the railing to get a glimpse of Fremantle and the beginning of their new lives.

Beyond the port, the land was flat and brown. The benefit of migrating from a rural enclave populated with friends and family to a town of brick houses populated by strangers was hard to comprehend for a child. But my parents saw what Australia lacked: the signs posted at every junction telling individuals of every race group where to stand, where to eat and where to sleep.

Years later, while attending the University of Western Australia and getting the education denied to my family by economics and the apartheid laws, I'd argue the existence of God with my grandmother. Cradled by the comforts of my first-world life, I'd point out the fallacy of believing in a superior being with a personal interest in our lives. My grandmother's standard answer was, 'If there isn't a God then you tell me how I ended up living here in Australia instead of back in the boondocks with nothing?' If I expressed a desire for the taste of a mango picked straight from the tree or remembered the spectacular thunderstorms that lit the hilltops with lightning, my grandmother would say, 'I'm glad I'm not back there hoeing the corn fields, my girl.'

She was unsentimental about Southern Africa. She agreed with an aunt who expressed zero interest in returning to Swaziland: 'All I needed from that country, I packed in my bags when I left.' During her final days in a suburban house at the end of a neat cul-de-sac in Beechboro, Western Australia, I wondered if my grandmother longed for a flame tree outside her bedroom window instead of a wattle. Perth's skies are wide and bright but they are not African skies. The air around my grandmother's house smelled of eucalyptus leaves instead of rain-soaked earth and bruised grass. Now, at the last, did my grandmother long for 'home'?

Possibly, but not enough to change the plans she'd already made for her final rest.

Like other migrants who'd lived through war and poverty, my grandmother had a prepaid funeral plot. It was situated further south, part of a large expanse of lawn with brass plaques set into the ground instead of headstones. Kangaroos ate the flowers left on the graves. Grass trees, once called 'black boys' before political correctness robbed them of that evocative name, stabbed their long stems skyward. Crows and cockatoos called from the trees. My grandmother had visited this memorial park when she was well, saw that it was not Africa and said, 'It's lovely. I'll rest here.'

The afternoon the funeral-home attendants carried her body out to the hearse, my aunts and uncles sang 'Senzenina' in two-part harmony. The younger of us, familiar with the mournful protest song but unused to singing it, joined in. The hearse took a right turn and disappeared into the sprawl of red-tiled houses and manicured lawns.

Life continued. Children rode bikes on the pavement. Electric heaters hummed behind closed windows, fed by a reliable energy supply.

My grandmother was gone. The sense of loss went deeper than grief at the death of a loved one, though that went plenty deep. My 'African-ness' seemed diminished: I was more Australian and less African without her. My rural Swazi childhood was a memory, fast receding in life's rear-view mirror. Australia was home and Southern Africa became a place to visit. This was as my grandmother wished it.

She adored air-conditioned shopping malls and chunky, wraparound sunglasses from the chemist. Perth's paved streets, stocked supermarket shelves and dry parks planted with dusty rose beds represented order and safety. Suburban living was sedate, but never boring. Walking through the front entrance of a department store instead of through the dingy 'non-whites' door provided her with thrills enough. Sitting in a front seat on a bus without an inspector demanding race identification papers easily compensated for the lack of fresh mangoes. Relinquishing the memory of Southern Africa's hot-earth scent in exchange for Australia's freedom of movement and anonymity was a price worth paying.

Two weeks after her funeral I was back in Sydney, caught in traffic and feeling a nostalgic longing for my African childhood. Memories of hunting grasshoppers through the lush summer grass and of playing in the fields till sunset took on a visceral edge. I missed the lazy rivers and the sound of wood doves in the trees. I missed my grandmother. A few months later on a winter's morning, with my bright-haired, part-Jewish/Hungarian/Swazi/German son toddling behind me while I picked spinach from the garden I had planted, I had a 'migrant moment'. An hour later, this Swazi immigrant girl, armed with the education that her parents had sacrificed so much to give her, sat down and began to write.

Southern Africa was a sentence away. A lying Afrikaner, a Mozambican pornographer and a fractious mixed-race community split by secrets... I invented characters and locations without censoring myself. From the safety of an Australian suburb I disparaged the old apartheid regime and made light of the pseudo-science that underwrote its racial segregation laws. I wrote a crime novel that threw dirt on all the race groups. The police did not knock on my door, as they might have during my parents' day.

I miss Africa with all its beauty and danger. It has become the land of my imagination and will remain so. My grandmother's unanswered prayer wasn't a wish to keep us in Swaziland after all; it was a plea to keep us safe and together in a country that offered us freedom and anonymity. I know now that the great good fortune of leaving Southern Africa behind me to grow up in Perth is captured in the movement of my pen as it glides freely across this page.

AMY ESPESETH

Staying Away

From what I hear, Nichole's funeral was beautiful: lots of family and half her home church travelled from Wisconsin to Iowa to see her lying still. She'd requested songs of praise to be sung and 'I'll Fly Away' finished the service. Folks spoke of her testimony of faith and her certainty that even if she had not been healed, Jesus was still our Great Physician and the lover of her soul. Her parents wept as her brother spoke; her husband of just past one year was dazed and oddly silent. After not that many months of battling a cancer that should've been discovered earlier – if she hadn't been chaste; if we didn't have such a suspicion of doctors; if she hadn't been poor – Nichole was dead at thirty-eight. Together, our church mourned and rejoiced; they sang, 'When the shadows of this life have gone, I'll fly away. Like a bird from prison bars has flown, I'll fly away.' So far away from home, I sat and cried alone.

I wanted to return, but I would've missed the funeral anyway. The distance was too great. And I was worried: when my grandmother died, it was requested that I not attend, as my presence would be a distraction. The oceans

– both literal and figurative – between here and home, who I was then and who I am now, both infuriate and shield me. Not that Australia has insulated me entirely from death: my local friends and family have had their share of grief as well. But here, the dead are dead and the living bury them; there are tears and tea and then it's done. At home – with my people, at least – death is a time of sorrow but also of rejoicing. Funerals are occasions for folks to affirm their faith and testify to the joy they have in Christ. Death is feared but approached with calm resignation, and loss is meant to be tempered by the certainty we have in both resurrection and heaven.

I haven't been home in over a year; it'll probably be past two by the time I finally go. I've promised my family this Christmas, but whenever I say the words or think of the trip, my chest tightens and I feel the blood pulsing in my ears. I'm afraid to go home. Wisconsin's snow and ice aren't stopping me, nor is spending money I don't have on the same gruelling Melbourne-to-Wisconsin trip I've taken so often in my decade-plus as an expatriate. And it's not the reprobation I feel whenever I visit my former church. It's something else entirely. She isn't dead if I never go home.

I don't remember the first time I met Nichole. There isn't a time in my childhood I can recall that she wasn't my neighbour and friend. Her family lived next to mine – 'next' being a relative term in rural Wisconsin where farms spread far apart even friendly neighbours. My family's land was homesteaded in the 1800s; although we no longer kept a herd of dairy cows, the fields were leased to those that did, and my uncle kept up Grandma's barn just in case someone would someday fire up the milkers.

Nichole's family were almost our enemies: they had come to manage a turkey farm. Folks that could not hold onto their land through farming or leasing agreements had sold out to the industrial turkey producer that somehow now owned our town. The cornfields and pastures had been converted into factory farms: long silver sheds full of white turkeys, clucking all day and night, pecking and huddling together. The sides of the dirt roads that led from the packaging plant in town to the farms in the country were littered with yellow-white feathers, turkey shit, and the occasional whole dead bird.

Nichole's family was there to farm these turkeys. Her parents didn't have a farm of their own, but they weren't there to take ours. I must've been six or seven or thereabouts when they moved from another tiny town to my tiny town of Barron. My older sister – then about eight years old – was always very dutiful in sharing our faith, and she immediately asked the new girl, nine-year-old Nichole, if her family had a church. They did, but they were like us: Pentecostals with an old-fashioned, fundamentalist bent. That meant that even though we believed we weren't under the law, we kept it nonetheless. We spoke in tongues and struggled to keep ourselves clean of sin. For reasons I was never told, her family eventually moved from their tiny church to my tiny church of the Foursquare Gospel.

Nichole became not only my neighbour, but my sister in Christ. Our families were together almost every day. We'd start the week with Sunday-morning service, including congregational singing and a sermon from my other uncle. Sunday school was for memorising Bible verses. Sometimes we'd spend Sunday afternoons at the local nursing homes, followed by nights full of praise and worship in the sanctuary. Wednesday nights changed as we grew: in elementary school we earned sashes and pins for recitation, evangelism and good works; in middle school and high school, our youth group undertook missionary activities targeting nominal Christians, fellow students, unsuspecting folks in Chicago, the unsaved in Nicaragua and Guatemala and, always, the pre-born. We proudly had Bible study on Thursdays at high school. Fridays and Saturdays were filled with family events, sleepaway camps and youth rallies across the state and nation.

Nichole was a constant presence in my life at church and at school. After school, we'd leave behind the yellow school bus full of town kids. Nichole and I, along with her brother and my brother and sister, would walk the many miles home instead of riding. The boys would often stride ahead, busy investigating the piles of dirty feathers or examining roadkill raccoon or skunk on the road. Nichole, my sister and I would go slow, not rushing to get home to homework and chores. We'd share about our walk with the Lord and we'd plan for our futures: husbands, missionary ministries and babies

– always babies. Nichole had a mahogany hope chest full of embroidered towels and dainty lacework. She'd memorised the virtues of a Proverbs 31 woman: faith, marriage, mothering, health, service, finances, industry, homemaking, time and beauty. Nichole was subsumed in preparing to be a good wife; I was not. I was not very interested in being a girl at all.

But by my freshman year of high school – when I was fourteen – things had changed, practically overnight. I got contacts, breasts, a spot on the cheerleading squad, and a football player as a boyfriend. Still a devout Christian, I was dedicated to evangelism. Fridays in autumn, our youth group arranged a safe and virtuous after-football party. While Nichole would leave the bleachers early to set up the church, I'd try to convince my fellow cheerleaders that pop and pizza in the fellowship hall was cooler than beer and boys in the gravel pit. Sometimes we were successful, sometimes we weren't. We were often mocked for our faith, but I seemed to more easily straddle the divide between church and school than many of our youth group. Nichole was friendly and always well-liked, but I had started to approach the realm of 'the popular kids'. Sometimes I even missed Bible study to hang out with the jocks at their lockers. Instead of attending a church banquet with my sister, Nichole and her brother, I went to prom with my boyfriend. Dancing awkwardly in a modest dress, I wouldn't touch a drop of alcohol. That night, I felt beautiful; I felt happy.

Rumours regarding my virtue started somewhere

and grew until my youth group pastor felt compelled to confront me. I was insulted but also strangely honoured: people thought that I could move so far away from my faith that I would cast aside my virginity for a linesman. I started speaking some of the questions I'd always had weighing on my heart: why weren't women allowed to serve communion? Why would scientists deliberately misdate fossils? If others lived out there in the world – seeking happiness instead of holiness – why couldn't I? Even through international missions trips and anti-abortion rallies, through Bible College and being slain in the spirit, I asked and I wondered. I doubted. And as much as I loved the Lord, I somehow loved myself more. I eventually left the church. Nichole never did.

But we stayed in touch through it all. Nichole went to Bible College too, but unlike me she dedicated her life to full-time ministry, teaching and preaching. I met and rapidly married an Australian man travelling in the States; I knew him weeks at our engagement, months at our marriage. I immigrated to Australia soon after. Even though I moved so far from my home, Nichole still sent me cards and letters. Although she continued to share her faith, she never sent messages of condemnation, only love.

Once when I was visiting Wisconsin, in a tearful conversation over cups of hot water and lemon, Nichole asked me for forgiveness. A decade earlier, with mixed motivations of genuine concern and girlish jealousy, she'd gone to our youth pastor and repeated the accusations against my purity. She had carried this betrayal for years and was humbly asking if she could lay down the burden. I held my friend and wept for the love she had for me and the difficult way she was still living her life. Another decade later – when my Australian husband and I divorced and I was revealed as beyond backslidden, actually outside our faith now from such a sin – Nichole still remained my friend. She prayed for me when I met someone new, and I hoped love would eventually come to her.

And it did. Late in her life, at thirty-seven, Nichole finally married. She hadn't known him for long – weeks at their engagement, months at their marriage – but they both felt a certainty in their spirits. After a short while, her husband told her something was wrong; he'd been married before and he knew more of women and womanly things than Nichole did herself. When the request went out on the prayer chain, my mother and sister reported Nichole's illness to me: cervical cancer. They were concentrating their prayers on the retention of her fertility – Nichole wanted so badly to be a mother. But they were also praying that God would spare her life.

After months of chemotherapy, spiritual devotion, dietary adjustment and intensive prayer for healing, Nichole was preparing for surgery to remove the mass that threatened her life. That is the last time I saw Nichole – it's the last time I went home. My new partner and I flew around the world to see my family and to see my friend. We drove down from Wisconsin on the snow-covered roads to the famous covered bridges of Iowa. Nichole's husband was strangely agitated when he met us at the door and rushed us into the warmth of their home. She sat on their couch, skinny and weak, her blond hair cropped close to her scalp. Her blue eyes leapt up when she saw me even though she could not. I went to the couch and we held each other and wept. Nichole was glad, embraced me and welcomed me home. She told me I'd been away too long.

We went to a restaurant and ate together, reminiscing about our girlhoods and watching our men cautiously speak to each other. Her husband sulked, unhappy that all attention was not focused on him and his struggling children's ministry. When his pouting turned to barely contained anger, Nichole deftly placed a shaking hand on his arm and whispered a few words; I heard her say 'gracious'. He calmed and she smiled. As we left the restaurant, I noticed Nichole had bruises on the elbow her husband used to steer her. I couldn't say anything; when my contribution to her life consisted of but hours per year, what could I do? By then, anyway, we had arrived at her parents' home and they too welcomed me with open arms. I was relieved and surprised: after my divorce, her father had not spoken to me the last time I had returned home. He glanced awkwardly at me throughout the evening. But when it came time to pray as a family, her father touched my hand.

Her brother would not see me. They called and asked him several times, but he chose to stay home with his wife and the children I have never met. (This estrangement is something that happens; I chose that when I chose to walk away from my faith. I have little anger towards him, more sadness. My sister tells me I imagine these slights, but they are too numerous to ignore.) After a few hours of chatting at her parents' house, Nichole was tired and needed to rest.

We returned to her home to say goodbye. She spoke of my meeting her children someday and of her meeting mine. She spoke of her great faith in Jesus and asked if she could pray for me. As we held hands to pray, I told her that I loved her and would see her again soon. My partner and I returned to Wisconsin and then to Australia.

Two months later, despite all the medicine and all the prayer, Nichole died. I missed her funeral, but I sent a bouquet of white roses and red gerbera daisies – they matched her wedding bouquet. I'd also missed her wedding – of course – but the pictures my sister took had made me feel like I'd been there. And I feel as if I was there at her funeral, too; I know exactly what they said and what they sang. I know exactly how they feel, what they are telling themselves to try to make Nichole's death bearable.

But she did not die for anything great, not in childbirth or as a missionary smuggling Bibles into China. She was not tortured or killed for her faith. She didn't die for anything we'd been prepared for; her death did not accomplish anything. Yes, she was a beautiful example of sacrifice and joy, long-suffering, and love, always love. People close to her believe her life was sacrificed for Christ, as an example to others, as a tool of salvation. This is where I part company with my family, my church and my former faith. They believe she wasn't healed for a reason – known perhaps only to God, but glorious nonetheless. I know Nichole died because the cancer was discovered too late. While they cried at her funeral, I know they also rejoiced. I have nothing to console me, however; there is only sorrow here. This is when I deeply miss my family and my home. This is when I profoundly miss my faith.

If I never go home, she isn't dead. If I never get off the plane, she is still alive. Often, my sister sends notes of condolence, encouragement and faith to Nichole's mother, father, brother and husband. But the cards I've purchased will stay on my desk, blank and safe, with clean insides unmarred by my messy handwriting and grief. Instead, I choose to live in a dreamscape.

Nichole is standing in her kitchen in Iowa, arranging a jam jar of sunflowers. She's got a low, big belly that says someday soon she'll have a baby girl to match the little boy balanced on her hip. Her husband is a pastor, a strong man of God, faithful and true; he adores her above all others. Her home is lovely, decorated with handicrafts that speak of faith and heritage, and her brilliant eyes and smile welcome any visitors. When I knock on the door and she opens it, she says to me, again, like the last time, like always, 'I'm so glad you're home, Amy. Don't stay away for so long.'

ROANNA GONSALVES
The Patron Saint of Excess Baggage

A female Indian guru, finding herself lost in one of those remote and self-actualising parts of India where non-Indians go to find themselves, is said to have proclaimed deliriously, 'The history of all hitherto existing migration is the history of excess baggage.' The meaning of this proclamation, however, is presently unclear.

The Australian Quarantine Information Service (AQIS), on the other hand, is extremely clear, taking seriously its responsibility to protect Australia from live pests. It has on its website a list of everything you must declare for inspection when you enter Australia. For my family and friends, this list is seen as an ocean that must be crossed, not in a leaky boat, but with a full and fitting multi-pronged strategy.

Two of these prongs are:

> 1. Masalas must only be transported from India to Australia in powdered form, must only be red in colour, and must be sealed and labelled with a professional yet exotic-sounding company name, such as Kapoor and Sons Oriental Spice Trading Company Pty Ltd.

Traditional advice passed down from mother to aunty to neighbour to friend is that if chilli powder is seen to be professionally sealed and packed then customs won't make a fuss, and you can enjoy Indian-home-made vindaloo, sorpotel and malwani chicken from the comfort of your Australian home.

2. For any feni to be worth its bottle, it must be home-brewed in a village in Goa. While this adds to its value, it could also be perceived as a threat to Australia's biodiversity. So, to raise it above suspicion and bring it into the country every drop intact, all feni must be poured into plastic bottles, sealed with clear sticky tape, and labelled 'Rice Vinegar for Cooking'. Then you can enjoy such a high that even the most professionally produced Australian alcohol cannot give you, however full-bodied its palette, finish and price tag may be.

In this way, all pronged up and strategised, we bring with us our attachments to the places and cultures of our birth and reattach ourselves, this time to Australia. In so doing we become aware that while we see Australia as an idea to which we want to become attached, Australia reciprocates our seeing with a gaze of its own. As author, painter and art critic John Berger points out, 'Soon after we can see we are aware that we can also be seen.' We change from seeing ourselves as Indians to gradually seeing ourselves as Indian–Australians, while becoming aware that perhaps we continue to be seen as Indians by Australians. This web of glances and gazes back and forth prompts the question, what is an Indian? And, what is an Australian? And must these answers be fixed and definitive?

In the first minute of my first lunch with my first white Australian friend, I felt compelled to reveal that I was vegetarian. My new friend attributed this declaration of vegetarianism to my Indian background in a genuine attempt to be culturally sensitive, while at the same time displaying a cosmopolitan awareness that Indians are usually vegetarian. What remained hidden was that I was born on a planet called Strictly Non-Veg, ruled by a communion of shepherds with names like Valerian, Simon and Ivan. We are a tiny speck of a planet, existing among other planets in a galaxy called Strictly Veg. Our planet is commonly known as the Bombay Catholic community.

The concept and allure of vegetarian food begins and ends with lime pickle for most of the inhabitants of Strictly Non-Veg. This is one of the many topographical features that set us apart from the rest of our galaxy, from the rest of Hindu India, from vegetarians with names like Narendra, Lal Krishna, Devaragunda – names that resound with the hoof and thrust of the Hindu religious pantheon.

There are three other topographical features that

would immediately distinguish us as of Strictly Non-Veg origin from the rest of the galaxy if viewed from, say, somewhere near the Southern Cross. For one, our surnames are usually Portuguese, vestiges of an inventory that was thrust upon us during the long red era of Portuguese colonisation of parts of India. Our foremothers and forefathers resisted Portuguese colonisation long before the rest of India began to resist British colonisation, but we are still usually judged by the fact that we kept their names.

Secondly, while we eventually learn to speak other languages, not always badly, our first words as babies are always in English. We scream 'Help!' in English during a particularly bad nightmare; we count the interest earned on our fixed deposits using English numerals. The experience of growing up with broken English heavily accented by regional Indian languages – as is so often commented upon by writers of Indian origin growing up outside of India – is not part of the narrative of my generation within my community, however heavily accented our own English may be.

Thirdly, we stick to our monotheist Abrahamic faith, even singing with rock-solid belief 'Rise India, Thy Millions Lead and Follow Christ Thy King' as the Recessional hymn at Sunday Mass with no hint of irony or mischief. We too have a pantheon, like the Hindus, but they are a pantheon of saints, not gods. We garland them, light candles at their waxed feet, and barter our devotion in return for good health, good jobs and visas to migrate overseas. But, like other Christians, we reserve our adoration for the One True God. Because of this sinful threesome, we are often seen as incredibly foreign and extremely fake Indians by some of those from the planet of Strictly Veg.

The consequences of these perceptions have ricocheted right around our galaxy, have tagged other Christians in India, even though they are not from the Bombay Catholic community. A nun or three raped, a priest or ten murdered, a church or twenty vandalised – what are these but excess baggage that must be discarded in order to uphold Hindu Indian Culture and Tradition, while sending one's children to Catholic, English medium schools?

When I gaze back toward India, I see that attacks on churches are a daily event in Karnataka, the home state of my paternal grandparents. I see that in Orissa, Sister Meena Lalita Barwa – a Catholic nun who was gang-raped by members of a Hindu fundamentalist political party and paraded semi-naked through the streets during the Kandhamal riots against Christians in 2008 – is still seeking justice. I see that deadly communal riots in various parts of the country have been manufactured and sold for a price. I see India's Muslim communities still bleeding from the Gujarat genocide of 2002. Christians and Muslims are seen as fake by some of those from Strictly Veg. These people choose to ignore that Hindus are immigrants themselves. They choose to ignore the oppression of the original inhabitants of India, the pre-Dravidian aborigines. My gaze, like those of many others before me, unveils and shames. Still, I look.

Even though I come from the planet of Strictly Non-Veg, and I am culturally, if not spiritually, a Bombay Catholic, I eat vegetarian food simply because I can't bear the taste of meat. For other Bombay Catholics from the planet of Strictly Non-Veg, I have descended into a moron of the oxy kind who has lost all value. 'You eat the Body of Christ, don't you? So why can't you eat other bodies?' is an admonishment echoed by uncle and neighbour and friend. This sentiment is even shared by my culturally Hindu friend, from another planet in our galaxy called Less Strictly Veg, who once remarked that the only reason they made friends with Catholics was so that they could visit them at home and eat meat.

I am a vegetarian from the planet of Strictly Non-Veg, and this is my excess baggage. No amount of candles lit at the feet of any patron saint can change this. Does this double negation make me less foreign and less fake? Am I seen as more Indian by those from the planet of Strictly Veg? Despite my un-Indian name, am I seen as more Indian by Australians?

Recently, as I checked out the star anise in an Australian spice shop, I overheard the saleswoman offering some customers a special house blend of Australian spices.

She said the blend included Indigenous bush spices as well as Thai flavours to acknowledge the many Thai restaurants that service the area. Now, there are thousands of Australians of Thai heritage who live in Sydney, but the saleswoman's exclusion of the Thai Australian community – not least the people who own and serve in these restaurants, combined with the distinct inclusion of the Thai restaurants that provide an economic, cosmopolitan value-add to the area – is a typical manifestation of a white-nation mindset. Just like the orientalists of old, who created the 'Orient' based on their own imagined ideas of what the 'Orient' should be, with scant regard for the realities in Egypt, in India and elsewhere in 'the East', we currently have white nationalists who create an Australia based on what they imagine Australia to be, with scant regard for this country's multicultural 'Real' (to use a term from the work of Ghassan Hage).

This imaginary Australia is represented every day by the broader Australian media-scape, by strategically monocultural Australian television, film and main stage theatre, even though we know that Australian streets and dinner tables are so ethnically diverse they would make the good folk of Babel fame blush.

A white-Australian optometrist recently assumed that I, a Third-World-Looking Person (to use another Hage-ian term), was a non-native English speaker, and asked me with no hint of malice – or irony – 'Do you know the meaning of myopia?'

Like most immigrants, I see Australia as a first-world country. Like most immigrants, I would not have migrated here if it didn't offer affluence, English as the main language and a safe democracy built on solid land – bloodstained and stolen as it is. When I put on my bifocals, figuratively speaking, it is plain to see that in choosing to make Australia my home, I as an immigrant am complicit in the reproduction of inequality between Indigenous people and non-indigenous people. I am complicit in its shame. Is socio-political critique through the arts an effective enough GPS to navigate through this shame and transform our gazes into a more equitable society?

A few weeks ago, a muscular, white-Australian man entered my train compartment with his bicycle. The air of authority that his handlebar moustache exuded made me overlook his more humble white overalls stained by blue-collar work. His tightly wound-up demeanour, ready to spring into action and slap you if you so much as breathed too hard, gave him a youthful appearance, although in reality he could have been anywhere between fifty and seventy years old.

He sat down for a few minutes before jumping up again, disgruntled, mumbling to himself, and proceeded to pick up all the rubbish lying around him. He picked up a red drink can, plastic wrappers, paper bags, torn newspapers and a blob of chewing gum. Then, with all this rubbish in his arms, he sat down again next to his bicycle. There were two others in that compartment with me: a young white woman and a young, fellow Third-World-Looking (TWL) man. All of us glanced at him at different times, and it seemed like he took these glances as licences to speak.

'I'm the only one that does this, nobody else would ever do this! Pigs, disgusting pigs, the lot of them! Brought up in a trash can not a house, shouldn't be allowed in here!' he said loudly and angrily, restless in his seat, peppering his tirade and umpteen versions of it with choice expletives.

All the while, he looked at the three of us, especially at the young TWL man. I thought of the Australian Quarantine and Inspection Service momentarily and wondered whether their jurisdiction extended to Sydney trains, and if their definition of pests included human beings. That thought soon gave way, however, to a feeling of alarm over this increasingly hostile language. It reminded me of John Howard's notorious line that split this nation: 'We shall decide who comes into this country and the circumstances in which they come.' It also brought back ugly memories of the times when I have been told by strangers, 'Go back to where you came from', like many other migrants before and after me. I pretended to focus on reading the news on my mobile phone, then keyed in 000, ready to press 'Call' for the emergency number if things got ugly.

I noticed out of the corner of my eye that the TWL man was also focused on his phone, the slight tilt of his head betraying the fact that his body was alert to the movement of the man and his bike next to him. Then something happened that changed the atmosphere in that compartment. The TWL man, sick of or frightened by this hostile language, looked at the ranting man. Although he looked with wariness rather than defiance, the ranting man immediately stopped, and suddenly realising that he was the cause of the wariness on the young man's face, immediately said, 'Not you. Ah, not you, mate, I wasn't talking about you, wasn't talking about you at all.'

The young man smiled and with the slightest of nods went back to his phone, his body relaxing just that tiny bit to indicate relief. When the time came for the older man to get off, he stood up with the load of rubbish in his arms, and then, realising that he could either carry the rubbish or push his bike, said, 'Fuck them! I'm not carrying their shit around. They can bloody well do their jobs themselves!' He proceeded to dump the rubbish on the seat, and walked towards the doors. At this point the younger woman also got up, walked towards the door, and stood behind him. The older man saw this and with a dramatic bow and sweep of his hand, said to her, 'After you'.

In some perverse way I was glad that he didn't carry other people's excess baggage with him. I was glad that perhaps this time it was a conflict of class rather than race that was the cause of this short-lived hostility – and my anxiety – on a Sydney train. However, I was most glad to see the ongoing process of what it means to be Australian unfold in this exchange, its courteous undertones overshadowing its previous, perceived aggression. As he got off the train I wanted to run after the man and hug him. But I stayed put in my seat – lest I be seen as an Indian, fake and delirious, who really ought to travel to a remote and self-actualising part of the world, and find herself.

MICHELLE AUNG THIN
Backtracking

On a hot February afternoon, a week or two after I'd first arrived in Melbourne, a stranger on the St Kilda Road tram spun me a yarn. He must have overheard me asking for directions as I bought a ticket from the conductor. He was certainly intrigued by my accent.

'You a Yank?' he demanded from across the aisle, a man in his late sixties or early seventies. Beneath the broad brim of his felt hat, his eyes were lively, curious, and he was neat and trim in an RM Williams checked shirt. Despite the heat, he also wore a powder-blue woollen vest as if he were up from the country, dressed for town.

'Canadian,' I said, and he apologised as if I might be insulted by his mistake. Then, feeling an obligation to make it up to me, he took the vacant seat beside mine and began to point out places of interest as we passed them: the last few remaining grand mansions of St Kilda; the War Memorial; bluestone Army Barracks; the Botanical Gardens; the fish-and-chip-shop water wall outside of the National Gallery of Victoria.

We trundled north, heat bouncing off the tram's wooden panels until the air seemed glazed. When we crossed Princes Bridge, the Yarra River opened out beneath us. Sunshine glinted prettily on the water, the shoreline edged with boat sheds, a cafe, wharves, railway lines and the squat brick bulk of Flinders Street Railway Station.

'Do you see that?' My guide jabbed his finger at the window, his voice rising with excitement.

'What?' I asked, scanning the scene for something historic or venerable.

'Flinders Street Station,' he said, with triumph in his voice. 'She isn't meant to be there, you know. She was meant for Bombay. Someone in an office got the plans mixed up. She is in the wrong place.'

The sun in an unfamiliar position in the sky; bright light splitting the day at an alien angle; the air hot and yellow when it should have been cold and grey; and all around me voices with such long nasal vowels, every word sounded strange. I turned to smile at my guide.

'I know exactly how that station feels.'

I like the idea of a railway station lost in transit. It amuses me in the same way that naming a swimming pool after Harold Holt, the drowned Australian Prime Minister, does; or insisting that the eastern tip of busy Collins Street, with its skyscrapers and fast-food outlets, is the 'Paris End'. I can think of many novels and movies set in railway stations – after all, stories follow where people gather – but a story in which a railway station itself takes a journey is one to savour. It sticks in my mind and I don't even care that it's unlikely to be true:

I like the perversity of this yarn. A wandering railway station offers a scenic diversion from my daily mental landscape. A landmark in the wrong place easily becomes a landmark of the imagination (if you want to get there, don't be starting from here).

When I let my mind drift as I travel on the 10.59 from Clifton Hill, I get a little thrill as I pass through the dark brick tunnel that precedes Flinders Street Station's platform 1. Is it possible (only just) that I might alight in Mumbai and not Melbourne? To wade in the Arabian Sea? Eat an ice at the Breach Candy Swimming Club? My tour guide's finger jabbed not only at what we can see, but also at what might have been. His story was an invitation to see something more – to see 'double'.

Seeing 'double' is something I know how to do. I was born in Burma but grew up in Canada, emigrating with my parents when I was a young child. I have no memories of Asia, at least none based on my own sensory experience, but that land was as real to me as the blanket of snow in my backyard. Burma was conjured out of my parents' and grandmother's voices. Their whispered reports of scandalous behaviour while we kids did the washing up. Rollicking accounts of tiger hunts and midnight feasts torn from the pages of Kipling. Memories, too, of private railway carriages and tennis parties and snakes as thick as your arm.

In a recent essay about writers and their families, the Irish novelist Colm Tóibín reflects on how the desires and experiences of previous generations frame your own.

He quotes Conor Cruise O'Brien, who describes this past within the present as a 'twilight zone of time', a period that 'stretch[es] back for a generation or two before we were born...[and] never quite belongs to the rest of history.' This twilight zone is made up of the memories of parents and grandparents, anecdotes told to you by uncles and aunties and second cousins. Stories that feel so comfortable, so lived in, that you come to possess them yourself, 'incorporating [them] into [your] own life'. You learn the trick of inhabiting places you've never seen but can summon up at will. You learn that the past – other people's pasts – may not belong to history but instead belongs to you. All those stories are yours to plunder. You can take them out, one at a time, and try them on as you might try on the clothes your parents have resigned to the dress-up box. There you are in the mirror (or someone very like you), the vegetal scents of long-ago swirling about your ankles. My own family's stories and memories stretch backwards in time, across the Burmese military *coup d'état* in 1962, Burmese independence, the Second World War and colonial rule at its high point. They were not my memories but were told and retold so often that I absorbed them, sucked them up whole. It felt like I'd lived them.

Burma was important for me in another way, as well. Out of all us kids – my two brothers and my sister – I was the only child born there. The city of my birth, Rangoon, featured prominently in my parents' tales. It was where they were married, where they had a big house with servants and an orange dog named after Mao Zedong. That dog used to stand guard over my bassinet. He was loyal but fierce enough to frighten my mother. Mao was the pet we children longed for, but never had, growing up in Canada.

I basked in the reflected glory of the city of my birth. It lent me a geographic prestige very helpful in the serious and cutthroat business of cultivating the interest of useful adults, like teachers or the parents of friends. I guarded Rangoon jealously, made it mine and mine alone. A city built on stories just for me. Like an inappropriate birthday gift from a dotty old aunt or a curio handed down through the family. Something to be taken out and marvelled at in private. Sinister and delicious, fragile and fantastic.

When my guide on that tram pointed out the window to Flinders Street Station, I understood his excitement. I am well versed in seeing two places at once – West and East; new and old; bog-ordinary and impossibly exotic. But double vision is also double-edged. When you see double, committing to one place isn't so easy. It is hard to focus. There is always the possibility of a life lived somewhere else. 'Once upon a time' can spoil your here and now.

I have a writing friend who reckons I am preoccupied with the idea of place. He claims that whenever I read his work the first thing I comment on is its setting: the weather, the landscape, the rightness of hospitals and streets and zoos, living rooms and wallpapers. He has a point. I do take pleasure in the ways a writer wraps a place around her characters. I yearn for fantastic places, invented landscapes where I will lose myself, not just when I read, but when I write, too.

It wasn't until I'd been living in Melbourne for a few years that I finally began to write about Rangoon. Maybe that's because it is easier to invoke one hot place when you are in another, especially when all I'd really known in Canada was ice, snow and the sweetness of a hard-won northern summer – never a day over 33°C. On a hot day in Melbourne, the fug from Victoria Street's fishmongers and butchers, its grocers and haberdashers, could easily pass for Scott Market, Rangoon. The scent of frying onion, ginger and garlic are familiar not only from my Canadian childhood, but my father's stories of good things to eat in Burma. When I run along the Yarra River, the water roiling at my feet is just as brown as the Irrawaddy.

Or perhaps it is because, as again that guide on the tram pointed out, this is a city that imagines itself en route between London and Bombay, in a country on the Indian Ocean that is relentlessly Western in its outlook. Adrift, displaced.

Writing, too, is displacement. It moves you, literally separating you from the everyday. When I am working, I am forever preoccupied. Physically there, but a little absent too, even from those that I love. To write I must be in two places simultaneously, one that is and one that might be.

I remember what never happened, I feel the prickle of heat in a land where I've never been. An orange dog lopes towards me across a broad green lawn. A young man in a powder-blue woollen vest flashes me a grin. He is goggle-eyed with delight at the buildings, the trams, the trains, the people all around him on this, his first day in the big city. How could you not lose yourself to these things? How can you not be sidetracked by what might have been?

Losing yourself is both the pleasure and pain of displacement, bitter and sweet, yum and yuck. You learn to live with it, like all those memories of generations past. Displaced, I cannot help but pause to catch my bearings and halt the relentless forward momentum I've built up in my life. Displaced, I must change the way I see, touch, smell, taste and hear the world around me. My mother tongue is made strange. Because I see that light falls at a distinct angle that changes depending on where I am. Because I realise that it is I who has moved and not the sun.

My guide and I both stepped down from the tram at Flinders Street Station. I shook his hand and thanked him for his stories, then left him on the concourse. 'Good luck to you,' he called after me. Behind us, our tram pulled north towards the city.

The late afternoon light was soft and warm air shifted across my skin. I was meeting a friend for a drink. We were going to check out Melbourne's nightlife. I strolled along Swanston Street, past Flinders Street Station's entry gates, ticket collectors and newspaper stands. From this vantage point, the building sat easily on its foundations, not 'double' or alien or anything more than a train station already busy with passengers, commuters who'd knocked off early to miss the evening rush hour and were now focused on the journey home. I kept moving.

CHRIS FLYNN
Gun for Hire

It was always my intention to get the hell out of Dodge on the first stagecoach that came along. Belfast was a cowboy town, filled with twitchy gunslingers ready to drill holes in each other's heads (in some cases, quite literally with a drill) and I wanted no part of that culture. I was born in the most Protestant area of Northern Ireland and spent my childhood dreaming of the strange, foreign lands that I knew were out there. I had seen them in books and films, those places where no one cared if you were Catholic or Protestant, where men who had tortured and killed more people than Hannibal Lecter didn't walk free from prison as political parolees, only to throw themselves back into a frenzy of blood and violence, all the while grinning maniacally from ear to ear.

With the onset of adulthood I was a puff of dust as the hooves of my trusty steed carried me off into the sunset. No posse was raised to ride out after me. I had gotten away, ginger locks pulsating in the breeze. My identity as a Northern Irishman would fade the farther away I got, or so I thought. What I didn't know, in my youthful naivety, was that everywhere I went people would be fascinated with where I grew up, what I did there, what it was like and oh, what a lovely accent you have I could listen to you *all day*. In other words, everything I thought I was leaving behind was everything the new people I met wanted to hear about.

This was frustrating. How could I explain that I was not a product of my environment, that the Ireland they mythologised was far removed from the reality I detested? As soon as you step outside your home country, you're automatically promoted to 'representative' – 'ambassador', even. I did not want the job. I specifically did not want to be lumped in with the prevailing perception of what it meant to be typically Irish. I do not drink Guinness. I hate it. It tastes like blood. I do not like *Riverdance*. Michael Flatley is creepy, and all those beatific dancers clad in green lycra, clopping around a stage like extras in a bad Monty Python sketch make me cringe with embarrassment. I'm sure those aren't shoes they're wearing, but *hooves*. Also, no one had ever called me Irish before – and if they did, I went to great pains to point out that I was born in Northern Ireland, which is part of the United Kingdom and not the Republic of Ireland, and so I had a British passport but also an Irish one and what do you mean that makes no sense?

In the end I succumbed to a simplified version of my own backstory. I would tell people that yes, I was Irish, but whatever images that conjured in their heads were almost certainly in direct opposition to the man I was so let's just move on please and no, I don't like U2. Honestly, I don't.

So began the process of reinvention. After sojourns in France, the United States and Thailand, I found myself slipping comfortably into the life of an Australian as the new millennium began. It seemed an appropriate time to start from scratch, to erase the hopeless, hapless Flynn of yesteryear and launch the new, sleek, bald version of Flynn 2.0 into the void.

※

The most delicious aspect of reinventing oneself is that you can dip your toes into all the waters the previous version of you wouldn't dare swim in. The jobs I held down in Ireland were of the miserable, plodding, typical variety you might expect in that most downtrodden of nations – factory work, mostly, and medical experimentation. Weary of the production line and the cannula, I vowed to forge new employment horizons in Terra Australis. Unlike the Emerald Isle, in Australia the options were legion for a fresh-faced, slightly sunburnt, young Irish whippersnapper of dubious abilities.

The employment agency I signed up with took one look at my woeful curriculum vitae, in particular my vast experience in solving existential conundrums as a philosophy graduate, and told me they had just the position for someone of my intellect – garbage man.

While the moment would hardly have made my father proud, I was elated. It is virtually impossible to secure employment as a waste management specialist in Northern Ireland. That, my friends, is a closed shop. One week in Australia and I was already being invited into the inner echelons of power. If they'd told me there was a job available as prime minister and would I be interested in giving it a go, I couldn't have been more shocked. Suddenly I was in Aussie Disposals trying on my first pair of steel-toe-capped boots and looking forward to getting up at four o'clock in the morning (although by 'looking forward', I of course mean 'dreading like the plague').

On every morning except Mondays, I would find myself clinging to the back of a garbage truck watching the sunrise and feeling like the city was mine alone. The sun rose on Mondays too, except the streets of the bayside suburb where I worked would be thronged with ravers, at the end of their weekends and their tethers, spilling out from an all-night club. Pale, ghostly figures clutching half-empty bottles of water and blinking in the light, a sheen of sweat glistening on their faces as they watched me lift bins over my head like the Hulk and dump the contents (mostly McDonald's wrappers and stolen wallets) into the compactor. I must have seemed like an alien who had landed on their planet, which is quite close to how I felt.

As it turned out, garbage disposal was on the more normal end of the jobs I would secure during my first year in the Antipodes. My next place of employ was to be a pillow-stuffing factory. (That foam doesn't get in there by itself, you know.) I arrived to find the workplace in turmoil over footwear. All employees had been required by management to don steel-toe-capped boots (which I fortunately already possessed). This did not sit well with the majority of staff, who preferred sneakers. The issue, it seemed, surrounded workplace injuries, an unlikely argument in a factory where people worked with feathers and artificial fibres all day. I quickly loaned my strident voice to the workers – why should we wear steel-toe-capped boots, we cried? The answer: in case a ton of feathers fell on you.

Management lackeys pointed out the enormous bales of feathers teetering on the precarious frames that lined the factory walls. Each bale weighed a metric tonne. It was thus vital to protect our toes, clearly the most essential body part. In case of accident, they could be sent to my mother in a small box. Concerns about the delicate nature of my spinal column were dismissed. I was put to work stuffing pillowcases with artificial fibres, which involved me literally thrusting my arm inside an ancient machine that sucked the fibres from my fingertips. Each time I withdrew the limb, I expected to see blood spurting from a stump – but consoled myself with a quick glance down at my feet, comforted by the knowledge that my toes would be okay. I quit after a week.

Despite my best efforts at wiping the hard drive and installing Flynn 2.0, there were clearly a few bugs in the new operating system that would linger for years to come, irrespective of the software updates. Seven days in a pillow-stuffing factory on the edge of Melbourne – a place I would have no earthly business being unless I was dumping a body – were enough to make me understand I could not cast off the old me so easily.

I was unprepared for the nightmare that would be purchasing lunch. The milk bar down the road from the factory being the sole establishment where nourishment could be procured, and I use that term in the loosest possible sense, was the bane of my newfound existence. The only hot foodstuffs for sale were pies but I could not purchase one of these steaming treats, as the elderly woman behind the counter did not know what I was referring to when I said the word 'pie'. I was labouring under the foolish misapprehension that there were only so many ways to pronounce such a simple word, yet no matter how I varied my tone, she shook her head and told me that whatever it was I was asking her for, they didn't sell.

I quickly learnt this was because I was asking for a 'pie' – rather than a 'poy' – which came with or without 'sorce'. I spent that week wrapping my tongue around such insanely stupid mispronunciations, actually pretending to be an Aussie oik, but it was never going to last. I felt like an idiot, albeit one who had something to munch on at 'smoko'.

This endearing personality trait was soon discarded and I resorted to relying on one of the more traditional, dependable foods of my youth – good old, reliable chicken korma. I know, right? *So* Irish.

⁂

Sport in Ireland mostly consists of men punching each other, or striking each other with sticks. Rugby, Gaelic football and hurling are the mainstays, though hurling is unique. Imagine your typical Australian Rules Football match – burly men leaping high in the air to take a mark, goals kicked between two posts, a bit of pushing and shoving, some definitely-not-homosexual horseplay in the showers. Now, give each player a long piece of wood, something between a cricket bat and a hockey stick. Make the ball the size and hardness of a baseball. Stand back and enjoy the carnage. This is hurling.

The rough and tumble hurling, hockey and rugby games of my youth were hardly an appropriate preparation for the sport I was soon to become expert in, one I did not expect to become acquainted with on Australian shores – sumo wrestling. Through an unlikely series of events I found myself employed by a travelling fair, initially in charge of a spinning ride into which I strapped unsuspecting children. The Velcro straps had seen better days, and after several more rotund little'uns had broken free of their bonds while the ride was still in operation, I begged the boss to transfer me to something less litigious, an attraction where I was not likely to be struck in the face with a severed leg.

I was made referee on the sumo-wrestling game. This involved me zipping young adults into ridiculous sumo-wrestler fat suits, then wrenching them apart when they attempted to strangle or stomp on each other. Only a cursory knowledge of the rules was required. I spent most of my time breaking up the fights that erupted post-bout, when ribs and internal organs were not protected by a layer of fake sumo blubber. Incredibly, the boss wanted to branch out from school fêtes and run the game in nightclubs. Clipping children around the ears and telling them to stop crying and shake hands was all very well – I could manage that. But I did not relish the thought of coming between young men my own age, fuelled by vodka and Red Bull, trying to tear each other's faces off. I was forced to resign my commission as a referee and seek employment in another sporting arena. The Olympics were calling.

More specifically, a friend who owned a cafe in King's Cross was calling. He was in desperate need of assistance, as he expected a deluge of tourists to descend upon his establishment during the Olympics. He had just the job for me. I was to march the mean streets of the Cross dressed as a frill-necked lizard, handing out flyers for the cafe. I did not know the particulars of my employment until I reported for work and was handed a shimmering blue lycra bodysuit that left nothing to the imagination, a tail, flippers and a giant lizard head. My stunned expression could be clearly seen through the mouth of the beast.

It was not a successful venture. My main accomplishments were almost giving SBS newsreader Lee Lin Chin a heart attack ('Get away from me!' were her exact words) and becoming embroiled in a wrestling match with a drunken vagabond who insisted on stepping on my tail while exhorting me to 'get a real job'. As man and lizard rolled on the ground throwing punches, a small crowd formed to witness what must have been one of the more surreal fights they had seen – although this was King's Cross, so perhaps man vs lizard was a perfectly normal sight.

Clearly, none of this would ever have happened to me had I chosen to stay home. Even if such jobs had been advertised in the Irish classifieds, I would not have applied for fear of someone I knew seeing me making a fool of myself as a frill-necked lizard or sumo-wrestling referee – not to mention the shame of presenting my mother with a torn and bloodied lycra bodysuit. 'Someone step on your tail again, son?' Instead, I would surely have resigned myself to a lifetime in the VCR factory, which eventually would have become a DVD player factory, then a DVR factory. I would have retired aged sixty-five having been unable to crack the impenetrable fortress of a life worth living, nothing to boast about to my grandchildren except the ability to recite a string of outmoded electrical equipment acronyms.

And yet it did not seem unusual to secure jobs like these in Australia, where no one knew me and anything seemed possible. The possibility of reinvention is one of the reasons why people flock to Australian shores. Here, it doesn't matter who you used to be. It's about embracing what previously seemed improbable – impossible, even – as the limitless sky stretches out to kiss the distant horizon.

Flynn 2.0 managed to tear himself free from the skin of the old Flynn and become the person I had always quietly yearned to be, even if it meant undergoing a much stranger rite of passage than expected. Now, on the rare occasions when someone inquires as to my upbringing in Northern Ireland or remarks upon my accent, I am briefly jarred by the intrusion of a personality long since gone, an almost unrecognisable man who might as well be someone else entirely. The reinvention is utterly complete. I pause as I consider the stranger's query, wondering who they are talking about. After a confusing few moments I remember him but he's gone, just a ghost now, a spectre haunting the graveyard on Steel Toe-Capped Boot Hill.

DIANE ARMSTRONG

Cracker Night

On a cold May night in 1949, about a week after my parents and I arrived in Sydney, I stood outside our little cottage, gazing at the bonfire that blazed in the middle of our Bondi Junction back street. I was nine years old. I couldn't speak English yet, so the words I kept hearing – 'Empire Day' and 'Cracker Night' – didn't mean anything to me.

Although I had no idea what was going on, the scene resembled a carnival. Everyone was out in the street: children were running around whooping, laughing and letting off fireworks while their parents stood around the bonfire, joking and chatting.

They all seemed light-hearted and playful, even the adults. Observing them, I could sense a warm community spirit and an atmosphere of friendship – such a contrast to everything I'd ever experienced.

What I *had* experienced until then was relentless tension, anxiety and fear. My parents and I had just lived through the war in Poland; being Jewish, our lives had been in constant danger. To survive, my father had obtained false papers and we moved to a village where no one knew us so that we could pose as Catholics. Little as I was, I knew I must never reveal our real name, or speak about the past. For three traumatic years, my parents lived on the edge of an abyss, going to Mass on Sundays and struggling to conceal their identity. In spite of all their efforts, from the moment we arrived the villagers suspected that we were Jewish and continually threatened to denounce us to the Gestapo. If it hadn't been for the support of the village priest, who had befriended my parents, we wouldn't have survived.

Although I was too young to comprehend the danger we were in, I was aware of my parents' tense expressions and anxious faces. At a time when most children are spontaneous and carefree, I was so subdued and apprehensive that I looked anxiously at my parents each time before I spoke, to ensure I didn't give any secrets away. By the time we arrived in Australia, I had learnt to be wary, and to keep my thoughts and feelings to myself.

So on my first Cracker Night, I stood apart from the others and watched from a safe distance. Shortly before leaving Poland I'd read *Alice in Wonderland*, and as the fireworks flashed and exploded, the soaring rockets, spinning Catherine wheels and glittering sparklers sent arabesques of light into the night sky. I felt as if I had stepped through a magic mirror, from a grey world of fear and darkness into an enchanted land of fun and colour.

One of our Australian neighbours, who had been throwing twigs onto the bonfire, turned and saw me standing timidly inside our front gate. Lighting a sparkler that crackled as it sent tiny flashing stars into the air, he came towards me. 'Would you like to hold it, love?' he asked in a kind voice. Overcoming my shyness, I stretched out my hand to take the magic wand, which seemed to be my passport to this new wonderland.

That night has come to symbolise the beginning of my transition from the old world to the new, and my gradual transformation from a withdrawn Polish child to a confident, fun-loving Australian girl.

It was a slow process. Although I longed to be like the other girls in my class, everything about me was different – from the leather satchel I carried to school to the strong-smelling rye bread sandwiches my mother made me, filled with salami and pickled cucumbers, while my classmates ate dainty white triangles spread with Velveeta or Vegemite. My long, unpronounceable Polish surname didn't help either. My face burned whenever my name was read out in class, and when thirty children swivelled around to stare at me with incredulous faces, I wished I could disappear.

On my first day at school, when the teacher said 'Next', a boy stood up, and I assumed this was his name. As soon as he sat down, she said it again, and another boy stood up. I was puzzled. This was obviously a very strange country, where all the boys were called Next. But the third time the teacher said 'Next', a girl stood up. I had learnt my first English word.

As soon as I could speak a little English, I was mortified whenever my parents spoke Polish in the street or in the tram because of the disapproving looks foreign languages attracted. Just as Australia was beginning to transform me, the arrival of thousands of European boat people like us had begun to transform Australia from an ethnically homogeneous Anglo-Celtic society to a more diverse multicultural one. We were engaged in what was really a collision of cultures. Many Australians regarded us 'bloody reffos' with resentment, suspicion and mistrust. We were threatening their comfortable, familiar world with our foreign jabbering, peculiar food and strange ways, and they wished we'd go back to where we'd come from.

Although I was impatient to fit in with Australian rules, I often had problems fitting in with my parents' expectations as well. My father, who was still steeped in the values his parents had inculcated into him, believed that well brought-up children didn't play in the street, so in the afternoons when my schoolmates played hopscotch, rounders and chasings outside, I wasn't allowed to join them. I resented being restricted by his old-fashioned Polish ideas.

It seemed that Australian children were far more familiar with their parents, too, and I envied the easy-going relationship my Australian friends had with their parents, who never seemed offended by their playful repartee. But whenever I repeated the expressions they used, my father was shocked by what he considered my lack of respect. 'You don't call parents *silly*,' he would rebuke me.

History lessons in primary school were another area of conflict, as my parents often had completely different interpretations of past events to those of my teachers. Whenever I enthused about the heroic exploits of the Elizabethan sea-dogs against the Spanish buccaneers, my parents would scoff that Raleigh and Drake were no better than pirates themselves. When the teacher extolled the altruism of the British Empire, my parents would point out that Britain exploited its colonies for its own financial gain. If I accepted their view of history and repeated it at school, I was ridiculed and howled down. I discovered that it was wiser to keep these subversive thoughts to myself, but it gave me an insight into the pursuit of historical truth. It taught me that cultural and national perspectives played a large role in the interpretation of past events, which is probably where my lifelong passion for history began. But as a child, these discussions left me straddling two worlds, unable to feel totally comfortable in either of them.

While I was struggling with these conflicting perspectives, my parents were confronting struggles of their own. Between them, they had lost over sixty relatives during the Holocaust, including their mothers, fathers, sisters, brothers, aunts, uncles and cousins. Of my mother's family, only she and one sister survived.

My father had been a dentist in Poland for twenty-five years. By the time we arrived in Sydney, he was compelled to study dentistry all over again, this time in a foreign language. Night after night, I would see him hunched over his desk, poring over his lecture notes while he consulted his English–Polish dictionary. He was looking up words he'd written during lectures, but as English is not a phonetic language, most of the words he'd written phonetically didn't exist.

While he was studying, my mother supported us by hemming skirts, jackets and dresses in a clothing factory. At the end of her day, she would lug piles of clothes home on the tram, and night after night she would sit by the faint light of our lamp, hemming and stitching. I can still hear the clicking of her heels as she turned the corner into our street every afternoon. Footsteps are as individual as fingerprints, and her short, rapid steps crackled with energy and tapped out a message of optimism for the future.

Despite their hardships, and their scepticism about the altruistic motives of the British Empire, my parents were unequivocally enthusiastic about Australia. My father never criticised the system that obliged him to study again, nor did he blame the Australian government for not helping migrants financially. My parents were grateful to be here, and couldn't get over the tolerance and kindness of our neighbours, who included me in their annual picnics, birthday parties and Tuesday night Physical Culture classes at the local Baptist church. As the pianist thumped out marching tunes on the tinny old piano, we learnt to move rhythmically to the music, and with each step I moved closer to becoming an Australian schoolgirl.

My father was impressed by Australia's egalitarianism and lost no opportunity to make me appreciate our new home. 'This is a wonderful country, where an engine driver can become Prime Minister, and the plumber is considered as good as the politician,' he used to marvel. Many years later, after my father had died, I was going through his papers when I came across the copy of a letter he had sent to the then Minister for Immigration, Mr Harold Holt. We had just become naturalised and he wrote to thank the minister, and the government, for accepting him as an Australian. He regarded it as a privilege and an honour, of which he was very proud. He meant every word.

Perhaps because the real world created considerable confusion and ambivalence in me, I sought refuge in the exciting world of books and girls' magazines. Real life meant worrying whether my father would pass his exams, whether my mother earned enough money to support us, and whether I would fit in at school, so the stories provided a welcome escape. Every Monday afternoon on my way home from school, my best friend Mary and I would rush to the corner newsagent to buy the latest copy of *The School Friend* or *Girls' Crystal*.

Sustained by a steady diet of detective stories in which suspicious characters were detected and exposed by intrepid schoolgirls, I lived in the hope of uncovering and solving a mystery, and becoming a real-life heroine. My determination paid off when, after a great deal of snooping, eavesdropping and misinterpretation, I became convinced that I'd stumbled on a criminal plot. Unless I took matters into my own hands, two girls in my class would kidnap another girl. By then I'd been made school captain, and as I took my responsibilities very seriously, I knew that I must reveal what I knew to someone in authority.

Filled with the importance of my mission, I wrote a detailed letter to the headmistress, alerting her to the fact that one of my classmates was in great danger. A few days later, I was summoned to the headmistress's office. To her eternal credit, Miss Child did not ridicule me or dismiss my outrageous allegation. She didn't question my sanity. Treating me with the utmost respect, she thanked me gravely for my concern, and promised to look into the matter. Reassured that the plotters would now be investigated, I was content to leave the matter in Miss Child's capable hands.

With my overactive imagination and my love of books, it's little wonder that in my adult life I became a novelist. And it's not surprising that Cracker Night, which had made such a powerful impact on me, inspired my latest novel, *Empire Day*. I set the story in the late 1940s, a significant period for Australia, when the influx of European refugees like my parents and me created a collision of cultures. The novel opens on Cracker Night, the evening when a kind neighbour held out a lighted sparkler to a little Polish girl who stretched out a hesitant hand to grasp her happy future.

GHASSAN HAGE
On Other Belongings

I was heading to a birthday party in western NSW with my wife and daughters when we drove past Bathurst. My grandparents had arrived there in the late 1930s and opened a clothing factory. My mother went to school, and then began helping her parents run the factory. She has good memories of many years spent zigzagging NSW in the family Studebaker as she delivered clothes to shops across Bathurst and as far afield as Lithgow and Young.

But in the mid 1950s, when she was thirty, my mother left Australia for Lebanon. I'm not sure if she did so specifically to find herself a husband, but she says she was introduced to my father – an influential gendarmerie officer at the time – fell in love, and stayed.

Although I never visited Australia as a youth, Bathurst was a familiar name to me. It was often on my mother's lips. It was the sender's address of the many large boxes that came by ship to Beirut's port; inside, among many other things, were those furry koala and kangaroo toys that were everywhere in our house. These clearly marked our household's Australian connections. So did the distinctness of my mother's accent when speaking

English. I remember Carla, the blonde German–Lebanese neighbour (and the secret object of my passions in my early teens) asking me, 'Why does your mother always say "aahy" instead of "eehy"?'

But far more important to me than the stuffed toys or the accent were the pictures of my grandparents in Bathurst that my mother kept in her drawer, which I took out and examined carefully every now and then. It was primarily these photos that constituted the portal through which I started to imagine what life in Australia was like.

The adventures of Sandy and his friend Hoppy the kangaroo in my favourite French comic journal, *Spirou*, helped extend my imagining. Courtesy of the excellent drawings of Willy Lambil, the series' Belgian creator, Sandy and Hoppy were my first introduction to images of the Australian outback and its culture, albeit in a clichéd, European way.

Sandy and Hoppy's adventures happened in various places, although mostly somewhere on the border between Victoria and NSW: *Poursuite sur la Murray* (Pursuit on the Murray) was the title of one suspenseful adventure. Yet somehow these drawings fused with the family photos to create my own particular idea of Bathurst.

When I finally came to Australia during the Lebanese civil war, I lived in Sydney but visited my grandparents in Bathurst. By then, they were old. The clothing factory was no more and all that remained was a frock shop that my grandmother kept going to make a few dollars that she spent during short telephone conversations with what was referred to, quite obscurely to me, as 'the bookmaker'. Soon after I arrived, my grandparents sold the Bathurst house and shop and moved to Sydney, where their children could look after them.

Despite having visited the Bathurst house several times, I had no memory of it twenty-five years later when we stopped on our way to that birthday party in Cowra. This is not surprising as I spent much of my first couple of years in Australia almost totally detached from reality. My most distinct feeling was of living in a state of suspension, produced by an acute sense not only of displacement but also of directionlessness. As a kid I dreamt of what it was like to be in Australia, but never with a desire to live there. Australia was simply not in a zone where I envisaged my life would unfold. In the back of my mind was a pre-Galilean image: the earth was flat and soon after people got to Australia they would start falling off a gigantic cliff.

So when my parents insisted I go to Australia to escape the civil war in Lebanon and continue my university education, I felt I was positioned at the edge of the universe, with no task other than to wait for... whatever.

This made Australia, for me, a transitional space unsuitable for purpose of settlement or long-term planning: what French sociologist Pierre Bourdieu calls a space of 'zero social gravity'. For Bourdieu, if one has no interest in the social reality in which one exists, then reality in turn fails to impose itself on one's senses and fails to pull one in. Reality loses its importance, and because of this, it loses its consistency, and even the materiality of the physical environment diminishes.

This was certainly the way I experienced Australia to begin with, and more so Bathurst. It did not really leave much of an imprint in my mind. I did not particularly miss anything about Bathurst when I stopped visiting. But on that day, on our way to Cowra, my wife Caroline and the kids were eager to see where Teita (Granny) grew up.

So I tried to locate the house, remembering that it was towards the Mount Panorama side of a long shopping street. Indeed, with Mount Panorama in sight, it was not hard to locate what to me clearly looked like the house. Next to it, I was almost certain, stood my grandmother's old frock shop. Nonetheless, I still had some doubts, and when we all got out of the car I was still trying to convince myself that I was not mistaken about it all. That's when a woman came out of the shop, locking the door behind her. She was about to go down the street but she noticed us all standing there.

'Are you looking for something, love?' she said.

'Is that the Debs' house?' I replied. (Debs is my mother's maiden name.)

'Well, yes,' she said, 'but it hasn't been the Debs' house for a very long time.'

She inquired a bit more and I told her my mother had grown up there. She said she remembered her, then asked: 'Would you like to go in and have a look?'

'Yes, thank you,' said Caroline, before I had time to say anything.

And so we all went in and looked around. I could not remember a thing: not the house's layout, not the shop's interior – although we were told that nothing had changed – not the furniture, nothing. I was a bit disappointed. The woman even showed us some garments that were still there from 'Mrs Debs' time', but I was unaffected.

Then I went to the backyard, and there something quite spectacular happened to me. The backyard was unkempt. There was no lawn, but a chaotic entanglement of high and low vegetation. Nonetheless, there, amid the chaos, I could discern three unmistakable forms: a fig tree, an olive tree and a pomegranate tree – the holy Mediterranean trinity, or one of them, at least.

At the very sight of them a complex web of emotions as wild as the vegetation that was before my eyes welled in me. I glimpsed a moment in my past when my mother, sitting on a long chair in front of our beach house to the north of Beirut, was telling someone the story of how my grandmother had an argument with my grandfather because she felt that he was wasting his time insisting on planting these trees.

I am not sure why the sight of the trees affected me so much, especially since, even though I had no memory of it, I must have seen them before in my early visits. Perhaps because I am pulled by the social gravity of Australia, now that I am as seriously immersed and interested in Australia as can be. Or perhaps simply because I am older, more existential and more appreciative of whatever memory and feeling comes my way.

But the thought of me on my way from Sydney to Cowra, standing in the middle of this backyard in Bathurst, next to a couple of trees that my grandfather had planted more than fifty years ago, was awesome (as my teenage daughter would say). Roots, routes, Lebanon, family, the cosmos, Heidegger and much more, all came racing into my mind.

But among all of the above there was one feeling that was particularly discernible and that I want to highlight here: next to these very Lebanese trees, planted by my very Lebanese grandfather, I stood there feeling rooted *here*, feeling more Australian than ever. What was surprising about this feeling was not its paradoxical nature. Rather, it was how non-paradoxical – or to use the equivalent of paradox in the emotional realm, it was how non-ambivalent – this feeling of rootedness in Australia was.

The Lebanese trees did not make me feel Australian and Lebanese, although I do feel both at many moments of life. Nor did they make me feel torn between my Lebaneseness and my Australianness. They simply made me feel, as I said, more Australian.

Reflecting on this, I came to understand that this was because it was not the trees themselves or the presence of my grandfather in Bathurst that made me feel rooted there. If I had seen those trees simply as Lebanese trees on Australian soil, I probably would have felt nostalgic for Lebanon. But this was not the case. Nor did the trees represent a memory of my grandfather that would have carried me to the time when he lived there. What seemed to me to have been crucial to my experience was the memory of my grandfather planting the trees. It was the practice that symbolised a specific relation to the land that made me feel rooted. And the trees stood there as a metonymic extension of that practice and that relation.

Now, despite the elevating feeling that overwhelmed me, I knew Australia's history too well to forget that I was in a town that was at the heart of the white settlement of Australia. I was also in a backyard: as quintessentially Anglo a mode of marking and shaping and rooting oneself in the land as can be. So I was well aware that others have come at different times and, through their practices, rooted themselves in this space. And, of course, I am too politically correct, and proudly so, to have missed the fact that my Lebanese trees and the Anglo backyard in which they were planted were both on Aboriginal land.

So I was fully conscious at the time – indeed at the moment I was experiencing a high, admiring my grandfather's trees – of the colonial histories of violence, domination and appropriation, of heroism and overcoming, of resistance, defeat and perseverance that marks the land on which these trees have grown.

But, again, this awareness did not diminish the sense of rootedness they infused in me, for this was not – nor could it afford to be – a possessive rootedness that claimed monopoly over the space of its emergence. For many people, a greater sense of rootedness does not mean a sense of being locked in the ground, unable to move. On the contrary, roots often are paradoxically experienced like an extra pair of wings. And this was exactly how I experienced my trees. I felt them propelling me.

It is important to stop and fully comprehend what propelling means here. When we are pushed by a force, it can make us go forward. The same goes with a force that is propelling us. Yet there is one important difference: when we are propelled, the force that pushes us stays with us.

There, it seems to me, lies the importance and the power of the roots that I am referring to: they are not roots that keep you grounded, they are roots that stay with you as you move.

I want to emphasise this mode of rootedness and its positive character because in it I glimpsed not just a way of being rooted, but a mode of belonging that can stand in opposition to the narrow territorial way of being rooted I have referred to earlier, which has often generated sadness and paranoia.

The latter inherits colonialism's exclusivist mentality, which operates with an either/or logic: either my roots or yours; either this land is yours or mine; either you belong here or there; either you are sovereign or I am.

The experience of rootedness that I found so uplifting offers a different path. It is not an anti-colonial belonging, which pits the belonging of the colonised against that of the coloniser while conserving colonialism's either/or logic. Nor is it a post-colonialism, which prematurely sees colonial culture as something superseded.

If anything, it is a supra-counter-colonialism: it counters colonial culture from a space beyond it, showing us that another mode of belonging is possible.

OUYANG YU

When Shall We Get Back to Our Country?

Abandoning one's loved home to expatriate. – Virgil

The other day, on my way home from teaching classes in Melbourne, I met a student of mine who revealed that there was nothing more he wanted to do than migrate to Australia. In his early forties, more than fifteen years my junior, and from China, where he had managed a small company, this man had a determination that reminded me of mine in 1990, when both my wife and I had a secure job each, she working in a research institute and I, as a lecturer of English at Wuhan university in China. With one child aged six and work-unit provided accommodation, we were well off enough to be comfortable where we were.

And yet, in retrospect, something more than the stagnant political situation following the 4 June Incident in 1989, and what would have been facilely interpreted as the call of freedom from the West, had seemed to be at work. Earlier, at the same university, classmates of mine, and later, my young colleagues at work, had seemed to share a tacit view that getting stuck in one place for the rest of one's life would be the death of one, even if it was comfortable enough, financially and family-wise. The best solution, all seemed to agree, was to keep moving, from place to place, from job to job and, if possible, from country to country, rather than have a clear future laid out before one. In other words, chasing the impossible, the more difficult and, to be more exact, the not yet known, as I once put it in the following lines:

> all i want to say is
> go away
> my spring
> here this year, there next, and i know not where the
>   year after

My life, as that of many of my classmates and friends, was thus a series of self-imposed changes or challenges in the chase of the unknown, by constantly giving up on things in favour of the more unreal, the more unrealistic; moving from Wuhan to Shanghai and back to Wuhan again before I came to Australia, it was there, in or about 1992, that I found myself writing these lines that I would never have imagined myself doing back in China:

> in a season of self-exile in Australia
> I feel doubly alienated doubly illusioned
> the death of the old world has such weird attractions
> while the light of the new world has somehow
>   darkened

MONTREAL, CANADA, 1986

In April 1986, while in Montreal, Canada, as head interpreter for a visiting Chinese delegation working on the Three Gorges Dam, I learnt that I had been granted an interview at ECNU (East China Normal University) in Shanghai after I succeeded in passing the examination for my MA candidacy in English literature. I was overjoyed. I was eager to embark on an academic career as I had entertained hopes of pursuing literary studies in a university after I had obtained my BA in English and American literature. Would ECNU bypass the bureaucratic process of interviews and directly accept me into the MA program? I wired Shanghai and received a 'No'. My second disappointment came at the start of the interview in Shanghai, where I was told that they only had 'Australian literature' on offer, instead of the 'English literature' that I had wanted to go for because the professor I had chosen as my supervisor had fallen ill.

Much as I was disappointed by the news, I gave up on my good job as an interpreter and translator, and went for the unknown. At the end of three years in the Australian literature program, I did well enough to be offered a PhD scholarship in 1990, jointly by La Trobe University and the Australia–China Council. By then, I had already begun teaching English and American literature at Wuhan University; according to my contract, I was not allowed to leave for Australia unless I had served five years in Wuhan, even though the scholarship was due to expire in 1992.

SYDNEY, AUSTRALIA, 1992

It is a complicated enough story of how I managed to leave, but to put it simply, I was able to come to Melbourne in 1991 on the strength of my expatriate Grandfather 10, an air force commander in Taiwan, as the Chinese government had a policy in favour of people with overseas connections – particularly Taiwanese connections – with which one could be exempted from the aforesaid conditions. In mid-1992, Jieguang, Grandfather 10's son and my uncle (who was my senior by one year), wrote that he was visiting Sydney and wondered if I could go and meet him there. I agreed immediately, as this uncle of mine had helped me a great deal with paperwork proving our authentic relationship on behalf of his father. I did not fly to Sydney, as he had suggested; instead, I rode a Greyhound bus on an overnight trip that took more than ten hours, slightly to Jieguang's chagrin. He did not understand a PhD student's unspoken need to save: I had to take care of my wife and son, who had joined me in Melbourne in early 1992.

A few minutes before the scheduled time of departure, I went to the door of a long-distance coach and presented my ticket to the conductor, feeling sure that it was the right bus because I had checked and re-checked that the ticket number matched the bus number. The conductor took a look at my ticket and said: But it's not the right one. Go back and check.

That sent me flying, without giving it a second thought. Bag in hand, I ran as fast as my legs could carry me, into the hall and up the stairs to the first floor, throwing myself headlong, breathlessly, at the counter, with a question: But they said this was not the right ticket? Only to hear the nonchalant woman behind the window say, after a glance: I told you it's the right one!

I ran back, downstairs, across the floor and out into the open where I was told again, at the door of the bus, that it wasn't correct. There was only one minute left before the bus would set in motion, no time for reflection or argument. I ran back again. The same thing happened, for the woman told me, again, in her flat tone: But I told you it's the correct one!

Finally, when I reappeared at the door, panting, I was relieved that the guy took my ticket without a question and, tearing a corner of it off, let me in. It was not till I reached the middle section of the bus in search of my seat that I, casually turning my head back, caught an exchange of smiling glances between the conductor and the bus driver.

I can still remember the helpless anger that gripped me and nearly threw me off balance before I held it in check. I have been holding it in check ever since, not even revealing it to my uncle when we met in Sydney.

When Alex, an Australian writer friend of mine, suggested I make a complaint to the bus company because such things had badly reflected on Australia and Australians, I thought it over and decided not to. Perhaps it was the shame that held my tongue. Perhaps it was not worthwhile making a *mountain* out of such a funny *mole hill*, as the rest of the trip did go smoothly enough. Or perhaps, deep down, there was a realisation that it was the cost of migration that one had to pay. For whatever reason, I have not written about this experience until now and hardly ever talk about it, exactly why it stays so clear and unpleasant in my mind, like the journey of migration itself.

WUHAN, CHINA, 2005

In early 2005, I made a decision of my life: I had to go to China to find a job. Since graduating with a PhD in Australian literature a decade earlier, I had not had a decent job commensurate with my qualifications. I'd spent 1996 writing up application letters, which I sent to all Australian and New Zealand universities, as well as many overseas, and getting short-listed more than a dozen times in this country, until I realised that my kind of Australian doctor's degree was not worth a farthing, as I had to under-qualify myself for lower jobs. Coupled with my wrong face and facial skin, my literature degree effectively worked against me and ensured that I would be excluded from the Australian university system once and for all, and for life, however many publications I had and however good my English was. The getting of the degree, and of this wisdom, served as a second, and worse, practical joke that Australia, like this particular bus conductor and bus driver, had played on me. By 2005, when I was nearing fifty, I realised that I had to go to China if I wanted a professorship, for Australia would never give me one, no matter what I did.

My wife accompanied me on my journey back to China in search of the 'ship, the *professor*-ship, which I secured in no time, ironically thanks to the PhD I had earned in Australia. Thus began my existence as a double expat, living as a *waiguo zhuanjia* (foreign expert), disguised as an Australian citizen, with a visa renewable by the year. It was like returning home only to find that the home had shifted elsewhere, a foreigner in his native town.

Without thinking twice, when I received my three-year contract, I put down my part of the deal – ironically again – that I would prefer to work six months at the university and spend the rest of the time back in Australia, where I was no more than a freelance writer and translator. My situation half resembled that of Ezra Pound, as John Berryman describes it in *Ezra Pound: New Selected Poems and Translations*: 'seeking an official post where he could be used, and…failure to find one produced both the freedom and the inconsequence'.

At the time, I was aware that many Chinese intellectuals, failed by the Western system and lured by a greater freedom – cultural freedom – had chosen to go back to China and stay for the rest of their lives despite their respective foreign citizenships, which prompted me to write the following lines:

After many years of living a death
After many years of an impossible whiteness

> After many years of make-believe make-live and make-feel
> After many years of heart-death tooth-fall
> After many years of pursuing the shadow of perfiction
> You now offer this little message to move me
> Not to tears but to years of a wandering life recalled in bitterness, spent in vain

Unlike them, I have chosen the middle way of bilingual, bicultural and bilateral living, an ironic choice that defies logical reasoning, except that it better suits my temperament to be living in two places simultaneously, one physical and the other metaphysical, an expatriate existence that merges the real with the sub-real and surreal.

MELBOURNE, AUSTRALIA, 2011

The beginning of the fourth decade of my forays into Australian studies and Australia saw me busier than ever as a double expat. I, like a tree, have struck deep roots in Melbourne, so much so that I return and keep returning to these roots wherever I go, branching all over the sky in my flight routes that cover half the world; most of the times an expat in the air, some of the time commuting between Kingsbury and St Kilda where I teach daily translation classes, and the rest of the time writing endless poetry, in either Chinese or English, in hotel rooms scattered across cities of China:

'Macho Man' (Wuhan), 'Double Celebration' (Chongqing), 'Southern Capital' (Nanjing), 'Western Peace' (Xining), 'Precious Moral' (Guide, or more Chinesely, Gui De), 'Orchid City' (Lanzhou), 'Western Quiet' (Xi'an), 'Deep Creek' (Shenzhen) and 'Fragrant Harbour' (Hong Kong).

I have written over 700 Chinese poems and more than 300 English poems in 2011 alone, and more than 4000 since I came to Melbourne in 1991, an exuberance only a born expat is capable of producing.

HUANGGANG, CHINA, 2003

It is ironic enough that when Ouyang Ming, my younger brother, was put in prison for his belief in Falun Gong – until he was tortured to death in Huanggang, my hometown, on 20 August 2003 – I could not get any support from the Australian government because he was not an Australian citizen, even though he refused to let me try to bail him out of China into Australia, preferring instead to fight to the end. More than myself, he was a spiritual expat in his own country, where his belief was turned into a crime and he had to sacrifice his life for an existence in the afterlife as a pure expatriate, an experience that dwarfed mine.

Born to migrate, to be an eternal expat, I have now gone beyond physical migration as I take a metaphysical existence by expatriating in words, in the form of fiction and poetry as well as literary translation, including self-translations. My 2011 novel, *Loose: A Wild History*, dedicated to Ouyang Ming, has incorporated his story that inspired the telling.

There is no longer any need to explain the early mysteries or ironic twists, as the writer, when gone, can be traced back only to his writings that deal with a life lived from moment to moment, here and elsewhere; and writings that contain the essence of his experiences as a spiritual expatriate for whom a home is but a bed, findable anywhere in the world as long as the place makes him welcome.

NOW IN 2013

The other day, I was translating *Things I Didn't Know*, by Robert Hughes, an expat himself, when I stopped at the word 'Christmas-cracker'. It was not till I found its definition in a dictionary that I sighed to myself that, despite my over twenty years in Australia, I had never come into contact with such things. Have I been blind to things people of this country take for granted? Have I been living a life parallel to those of others with little interaction?

I am reminded of the fact that I have never spoken a single word to our neighbour – someone who looks like a Central European and regularly tends to his vegetable garden, sending forth a miscellany of smells that my wife complains about – nor he to me, over our fence. And I know, sadly, that we won't be speaking till we both depart from this world – a hard fact of Australia, more so than anywhere else, both of us expats in our own isolated ways, entrenched in a country in which we choose to live.

I was reading a Chinese book on Confucius on my way to work by tram, when I realised, for the first time in my life, that Confucius was an expatriate himself, wandering from state to state, preaching his teachings that, during his lifetime, never became valued for what they were. The Chinese word used to describe his wandering expatriation is *piaobo*, a verb that literally means to drift–anchor or that denotes a state of drifting–anchoring. In a sense, we, Confucius and I, are drifters who anchor in drifting and drift in anchoring, an eternal expatriate, a word that I could recreate as *expiaobotriate*.

'When shall I get back to my country?' My answer to the question by Ezra Pound in exile would be: Probably never, because I am already in my country, the one in my mind.

DANNY KATZ
The Crappiest Refugee

There are a fair number of politicians who want to turn this country into an insular, isolated, boat-rejecting, immigration-slashing, closed-bordered, closed-minded bastion of fortified *rackofff*-ness – and personally, I think that's an excellent thing.

I'm fully behind them, if only to keep out the Canadians.

I've got no problem with refugees coming here from Pakistan, Afghanistan or Kiwistan, but something must be done to curb the influx of Canadastanis flowing insidiously across our borders like thick maple syrup smothering a helpless little butterball atop a compassionate short-stack of pancakes.

Those Canadians, they're desperate to come here: they look at Australia and go, 'Oooh, it's so much like home, eh? Same laid-back lifestyle, eh? Same laconic humour, eh? I want to go to *there*, eh, ehhh, EHHH?' But when they get here they make no effort to assimilate like other refugees, or to immerse themselves into Australian society.

You see them walking our city streets in small,

intimidating caribou packs, offending everyone with their culturally insensitive Roots-brand Beaver Canoe sweatshirts. You see them working out in their suburban gymnasiums, flashing their repulsively overdeveloped moose-pecs and humming Nickelback songs unironically. You see them in our pancake eateries, throwing forks across the table in disgust and whining to waitresses, 'The *amberness* of this maple syrup does not appear to be of an acceptable 60.5 to 74.9 per cent translucency! If I'm not very much mistaken, this is *mock* maple! Bring me genuine maple syrup *immediately*, in a proper glass bottle with an impractically tiny handle for my impossibly brawny Canadian fingers!'

Yeah, yeah, here we go. All you lefties and greenies and Arnold Zable-ies are going to start prattling on about how we should accept asylum seekers of *every* nationality, how Canadians have fled lives of great hardship, suffering under the Taliban-like French–Canadian fundamentalists who brutally force supermarkets to have both English and French labelling on all their merchandise, so that 'ketchup' is also called 'ketchuppe'.

Or how Canadians have escaped the barbaric regime of Cirque du Soleil, who indoctrinate innocent young people and teach them to balance on tightropes while dressed as freaky ladyboy whore-clowns. It's so degrading. But how are we supposed to be compassionate when newly arrived Canadians insist on keeping their ethnic culture, language and religion? When they continue to walk around in public covered from head to toe in their traditional maple-leaf garments, so that they look like small, mobile botanical gardens? When they refuse to stop speaking in their native accents? Oh, they think they sound so sexy and transatlantic, but they don't – they sound like a drunken American chewing on a Mintie that's caught in the back of their retainer.

Deport the Canadians, I say. Send them back to T'rono.

But before you call me a hateful anti-Canuckist, let me confess something: I am a Canadian refugee myself! In the early 1970s my family fled Canada, crossing the seas on a decrepit old ship: a Qantas airship with no movies – and my window shade wouldn't go all the way down. I was smuggled into Australia under my father's lumberjack jacket, hidden in his burly Canadian chest-hair; my sister hidden in my mother's.

We began a new life of freedom here, but my parents refused to abandon the customs of their birth country. They made me walk around the streets in snowshoes, huge tennis-racket-shaped ones tied to each foot, in the middle of summer! Forced me to speak only Canadian around the house; insisted I eat imported Jell-O for dessert instead of locally sourced Aeroplane Jelly; and wouldn't let me sing the Australian national anthem around the house – it always had to be the Canadian anthem, Gordon Lightfoot's 'If You Could Read My Mind'.

Deport me.

Anti-assimilation was hardwired into me. When I started primary school, I hung desperately onto my heritage, half out of loyalty to the ancient ways of a proud people, half because I was an unremarkable, un-sporty little dweeb, and the only gift I had with which to impress other kids at school was that I came from Canada and nobody at school quite knew what a 'Canada' was.

I was quite exotic and mysterious, in a bland, white-bread way. Every day at recess and lunchtime I would regale my classmates with enthralling tales of my rugged upbringing in the desolate wilderness of suburban Toronto: how the kids there rode to school on moose; how my dad was a lumberjack (*and he's okay, he works all night and he sleeps all day*) and my mum a Royal Canadian Mounted Policeman (she actually worked in the *same* department as Dudley Do-Right); how my ten-year-old sister played professional ice hockey at a centre for the Toronto Maple Leafs and how on weekends I went out and clubbed baby seals for their fur.

Deport me.

Then when high school started I still refused to let go of my natural Canuckisms, even if Gregory Rugless tried to beat them out of me on the first day, throwing me down onto the asphalt and sitting on my chest with his knees pinning my arms, yelling into my face.

'You from America, then?'

'No, I'm from Canada.'

'You sound like a Yank, poofter.'

'No, I come from Canada!'

'There's no such place as *Ca-nay-dee-ya*!'

'Yes there is such a place – a righteous, wondrous place – and it's not pronounced Ca-nay-dee-ya, you disrespectful muskrat! It's CAH-NAH-DAAAH!'

Then he gave me a titty-twister for my arrogance – a 360-degree, full-nipple rotation.

This brutal persecution just made me more resolute than ever: I would NEVER betray my homeland and become one of THEM. I would never go to the school tuckshop and ask for 'to-MAH-toe sauce on me pie' in that drawly Aussie way. If I was at the school canteen, I insisted on calling it by its rightful name: 'Could I have to-MAY-toe ketchup, *merci beaucoup?* Yes, just distribute it on the top of my pastry stuffed with indeterminate meat stuffs, thank you Barbara, kindly old canteen lady.'

There was also no way I would ever take a bite of pavlova at friends' houses: that stuff was disgusting – it was like biting into a Styrofoam cup filled with shaving cream. Never would I call another boy 'maaate'; it just didn't seem right, seeing that we weren't actually mating. (And they are flip-flops by the way, not thongs. They are *flip-frickin-flops*.)

Those teen years were a painful time for me: I became a lonely, downtrodden outsider. How I pined for my home and native land, Oh Ca-nay-dee-ya.

Deport me!

You'd think I'd have broken by the end of my teens. You'd think I'd have fallen to my knees like an ice-hockey goalie deflecting a puck, howling 'Okay, I relent, stuff me full of Iced VoVos and AUSSIFY ME, *MAAAAAAAATE*...' But nuh-uh, no way, hosers: throughout my university years I remained stubborn and unyielding, if only because my Canadian-ness turned out to be the only quality I possessed that made any woman ever actually want to communicate with me. When I started uni I was hopeless around women, since I'd spent the previous six years at an all-boys high school where the closest thing I had to female flirtation was Old Barbara the Tuckshop Lady asking if I wanted my finger bun buttered.

But suddenly girls seemed interested: one lunchtime I was in the student union cafe, ordering food in my over-friendly foreign tongue ('Can I have po-tayyy-toe chips with to-mayyy-toe ketchup on them, fine gentleman? And throw in this bottle of soda pop, please.') and the girl standing behind me said, 'Oh I love your accent, where are you from?' and I said 'I'm from Canada', and she said, 'Say something to me in your accent', and I just stood there for two minutes going, 'Umm... Whaddya want me to say? Umm... I don't know what to say', because it's almost impossible to think of something to say when people ask you to say something. She said, 'Just say "out and about"?', and I said, 'Why do you want me to say "out and about"?' – but as soon as I said 'out and about', she started laughing hysterically and mimicking me, saying 'oot and aboot, oot and aboot', which is apparently how I said it, although I don't think I sounded that ridiculous. But I didn't get mad with her and I didn't make a fuss, because I wanted to have sex with her at some point in the future. So I just stood there, grinning like an idiot, saying 'ooot and abooot'.

Without any shame I admit it: I used my Canadian-ness for wickedness, seducing your naive, fetching Aussie women by laying on a super-thick, super-sexy Michael Bublé accent. 'BANANA' turned into 'BA-NANNN-NERRR' and 'PYJAMA' was amped up to 'PEEEE-JAMMM-ARRRS', as in, 'Hey babe, why don't you have another sip of your BA-NANNN-ERRR daiquiri, and take off your PEEE-JAMMM-ARRRS, and let's get ooot and abooot, ehhh?' I dabbled in Extreme Canadian-ness around campus, breaking hearts with my shoulderblade-lashing Wayne Gretzky mullet. Wearing my hyper-manly flannelette shirt (and matching raccoon hat). And playing my guitar on the library lawn, singing Canadian songs by Neil Young, Joni Mitchell and the legend that is Bryan Adams.

DEPORT MEEE!

Because I'm never going to change, I'm never going to succumb; all these years later I'm still hanging on, and why should I change when Australians seem to really love Canadians? They do, and I've no idea why. Maybe it's the simple fact that we're not Americans. Maybe it's our gentle, over-friendly manner. Or maybe it's the fact that just like Australia, Canada is an inoffensive, unthreatening, totally innocuous country with no geopolitical relevance whatsoever; if it disappeared tomorrow, it wouldn't make much difference to the great scheme of things – there'd just be fewer lacrosse tournaments and Mike Myers movies, so that could be good.

Even now, whenever I meet an Aussie and I say 'Hello' in my whiny, nasal Canadian accent, I see them automatically freeze up; they give me a long, suspicious stare and say, 'Are you American?' I always leave them waiting with a big dramatic pause, and then I let rip with a nauseatingly syrupy smile and say, 'No, actually I'm a Canadian', and instantly their anti-American, anti-imperialist, Yank-hating faces *MELT* into an expression of relief and utter adoration, and they say, 'Oh, I just *LOVE* Canadians', and they shake my hand and give me a hug, and ask me if I know their cousin Jennie who backpacked through Vancouver in the early 1990s, and I just nod my head and say, 'Of course I know Jennie, good ol' Jennie' – even though I don't know Jennie, I've never even been to Vancouver and I haven't lived in Canada since I was seven.

See what I'm saying? All those politicians are right, immigration numbers should be slashed – but let the genuine refugees in and, I beg you, just stop us Canadians at the border, because we will never make any attempts to integrate, to become true-blue like you. So here's what I'm demanding: I want the federal police to burst into my home as soon as possible and drag me out my door and throw me on a plane and fly me off to a detention centre in Nauru or East Timor or Malaysia – me and the only other Australian–Canadian who comes to mind: crime-writing literary supermodel Tara Moss. And together we should be detained indefinitely in a tiny, dark isolation cell in tropical temperatures with only one set of clothes and a single-bed mattress.

Do that to me, Australia. I deserve it.

MARK DAPIN

Nineteen Eighty-Eight

There was nothing left for me in England in 1988.

My birthplace, the northern city of Leeds, was the cemetery where my father was buried, and my grandfather lay in a hospice, waiting to die. I'd long ago ceased to call it home. I couldn't speak with a Yorkshire accent anymore. I'd had the rounded vowels chased out of me when I was twelve years old and moved south with my mother to Aldershot, the sullen, Victorian 'home of the British Army'.

Our garrison town had a banal, violent glamour, and I disguised myself in its pikey-squaddie street-style, with rails of earrings and a skinpaper of cheap, gaudy tattoos. But tattoos aren't armour, and I was never tough enough to belong.

I did badly at a bad school, but I managed to matriculate, and found a place at the University of Warwick, in the Midlands, one of the few institutions that would accept a student without any kind of pass in Maths. I felt a part of life at Warwick, where each year the community was remade by a new intake of students.

I was slightly more worldly than some, and a bit younger than most, but the politics and drinking came easy to me, and I hoped they would go on forever.

But I missed out on a postgraduate place at university and, by bad luck and poor judgement, remained in the Midlands after I graduated. There were no jobs north of Luton in Thatcher's Britain, and I should have moved to London right away. In my imagination, I make that journey still, with reserves of courage, drive and imagination that I didn't possess when I was twenty-one years old, cynical and stoned, waiting for someone else's revolution.

I took money from government schemes designed to give experience to the long-term unemployed, but the jobs didn't need to be done, and I hardened against the idea of work. I lost my ambitions, and wished I had grown up instead in the 1950s or 1960s, when opportunities seemed to have been opening up rather than closing down; or the 1930s, when there was a real evil to fight, not just the blind vandalism of the spiteful elite.

My life changed when the value of my girlfriend Jo's house in Coventry suddenly doubled, and she sold up and split the profits with me.

We fled to South-East Asia, with Australian working-holiday visas in our passports. I had an aunt who lived on a hobby farm in Seymour, Victoria, who offered us a place to stay when we arrived in Australia in 1989. Auntie Gloria had left England many years before. She'd felt my grandparents were ashamed of her, an unmarried

Jewish girl. In Melbourne, she'd found a husband when she was already too old for children. She didn't see me as a son, but I was her closest nephew. She'd wanted to be a writer, too. One of her novels was almost published. She'd worked as a proofreader on the *Jerusalem Post*, then as a schoolteacher. By the time Jo and I arrived, she was living off her pensions on a property with cows and chickens and my Uncle Bill.

I knew nothing about Australia. My best mate had visited, but I'd only half listened to his stories of sailing and suntans. It sounded like a long, slow afternoon on the dole. Jo and I spent two weeks in Seymour, and the first Australian stranger we met – a fellow passenger on the train to Melbourne – invited us to her house for Christmas dinner. This wouldn't happen in Coventry – unless your host was planning to murder you – and it never occurred again in Australia. But there's a magic to migration that rewards you for even taking the first step.

In 1989, we had no plans to stay in Australia. England was still my home, and the home of the Sex Pistols and the Jam, Fred Perry shirts and Ben Sherman Originals, curry houses and corner pubs. I never cared about Australia's sunshine or beaches, and I was blind to its beauty. We moved to Sydney, where I immediately found a job as a proofreader in a typesetting shop. At twenty-six, I joined the world of permanent, full-time work.

I lied that I'd edited a free newspaper back in England, when in fact I'd worked for a month selling advertising – and never earned a penny's commission. But the man who hired me was impressed by my honours degree (although virtually all degrees are honours degrees in England) and my smart suit (which I'd recently had made for about $50 in Bangkok).

I reinvented myself on the spot, rewrote the wasted years, and ever since then my life has been more successful than I would ever have imagined in England in 1988. But I'd needed to leave home to make it happen. I had to leave myself behind. I could only do this in another country, where my background couldn't or wouldn't be checked.

I didn't miss England. My old friends visited. Some moved to Australia. Occasionally I would reminisce unconvincingly about cold weather and warm beer, but if I was ever nostalgic it was for a time and not a place. I would have liked to have been fifteen again, or twenty. These seemed to me to have been my glory years, when I knew I was happy. But that happiness returned to me in Australia, that sense of being on the edge of something exciting, when life was loaded with potential. I couldn't go home. I guess I feared that once I stepped off the plane, I'd lapse into the person I used to be. I still find it hard to imagine having a job in London, or buying a house, or being accepted, although I know in my heart it would come easily.

My grandfather had told me he'd wanted to move to New Zealand in 1948, but my grandmother wouldn't leave Leeds. My grandfather was like me – or, perhaps, I modelled myself on him. He enjoyed a drink – sometimes for days on end – and, when I grew older, I think we recognised each other through the bottom of a glass. He died four days after I left England, and then there was only me.

I think he probably had a lot he wanted to leave behind. He had been a Civil Defence Service rescue worker in World War II, a born East Ender dragging the broken bodies of his neighbours out of their shattered houses during the Blitz. He never spoke about the war: he just drank it down. I was trying to drown something more essential, but when I moved to Sydney I changed the person I was. I gave up smoking (several times) and quit drinking psychotically (except when I couldn't stop myself). I started to train at the gym, with weights and boxing gear. I filled out and I grew up. I put on a new mask, a new accent. I even – *almost* – convinced myself.

I started to think about being Jewish. At home, it had only been a handicap – like a broken leg or a lazy eye – that made me easier to hit. In Sydney, it seemed faintly exotic. For much of what might loosely be called my 'schooling' in Aldershot, I was the only Jewish boy in a single-sex state school where a large number of pupils came from army families. It was a difficult position for a clever kid and I dealt with it by ceasing to be clever – or rather, by turning my intelligence against the school.

But among the Australians I met in Sydney, there seemed to be no consciousness of Jewish people, or even religion. When I was the editor of a 'lads' magazine' called *Ralph*, a very bright and capable nineteen-year-old cadet journalist came into my office to ask if Jesus and God were the same person. And I'd been going out with my girlfriend for two years when she wondered out loud if Israel was a Christian or Muslim country.

I didn't embrace the Jewish religion – much less Zionism – but I began to look for my place in a historical continuum. My family history is complicated and confused. Large chunks of it have been deliberately forgotten. In their places are rumours of pogroms and massacres, flames that may never have burned. My great-grandfather was an English–Jewish dockworker of German ancestry. I was always told he had fought in the Boer War; I've seen a picture of him in military uniform, but I can't find his name on any record of men who served. I was brought up to believe his wife, a cigar-maker, was Spanish, but educated in France. Latterly, she has become Turkish, a Sephardic refugee taken in by the Ottoman Empire. My grandmother told me her parents came from 'Estonia, Latvia and Lithuania' – three countries for two people. She was never able to be more precise. On my father's side, both of my grandparents died before I was born, but I believe they – or their parents – fled pogroms in Minsk, in what is now Belarus. For generations, my ancestors moved across the next border when their homes burnt down, chased – at least in my imagination – by laughing bandits on horseback. I don't claim any parity of experience with them. I know my migration was trivial compared with theirs. But now that I have children, I worry a little that I might make the same mistakes as they did.

My great-grandmother's generation carried to England the ignorance of peasants. Gloria told about the time when the other Jewish women in the street surrounded my grandmother's house, petty pogromists in aprons and scarves, accusing my infant mother of putting 'the evil eye' on their babies.

My grandmother herself was a generation removed from an Old Country she could not even name, but both she and my grandfather clung to ancient ideas about 'marrying out'. My grandfather wouldn't talk to my mother for a year after she left my father for a *yok* (working-class Yiddish back-slang for *goy*, a non-Jew). He didn't actually board up her room at home, as custom dictates, but then he never was one to do unnecessary work around the house.

When their daughters were young, my grandparents did everything they could to prevent them from gaining an education, because they believed an educated woman was an unmarriageable woman – and somewhere, at some time, in some village south of Riga, Latvia, they probably would have been right. Some immigrants – perhaps especially perpetual immigrants, like the poorest Jews – find it hard to understand they have moved into a new society, as well as a new country; and impossible to accept that the things they have learnt in their lives no longer apply. I feel sad, as well as furious, when I read of ferocious patriarchs who murder or disfigure their daughters in the name of a family honour that has been rendered meaningless by their migration. A savage, clannish gangsterism might have protected them – and perhaps even their children – in a Balkan mountain redoubt, but it's just an evil sickness in south-western Sydney.

But I'm sometimes faintly frightened that in my mild, middle-class way, I'm not so different from them. Although I've been in Australia for twenty-two years, I try to equip my children to live *my childhood*. My seven-year-old son has been training in martial arts for four years, and my daughter started at three, but I have met many Australians who've never had a fight. It angers me to see my son wearing school uniform, but I know it reminds me of arbitrary discipline and an imitative militarism that's wholly outside the experience or ambitions of his teachers. I will not save for his secondary education, but I can see the left has collapsed, and privatisation and fee-paying schools are the way of the future. But I can't let go of those things I have always believed to be right. I can't compromise with reality. I can't imagine the world I see around me. It's not as real as the world in my head.

There was nothing left for me in England in 1988, but I fear I'll live there all my life.

DEBORAH CARLYON
Hidden by the Dream

My first night in Australia I dreamt I was watching an Aboriginal corroboree.

I was led by the flickering of fire through tall gum trees, bushes and vines. Crouching beneath a canopy of leaves, I remained hidden but I was not afraid. I was drawn closer by the movements of the tall and slender male dancers, their skin glistening beneath ochre clay and beads of sweat. Orange flames and white body paint were vivid, and I was breathing the breath of the dancers. In that fleeting moment between sleep and wakefulness, I somehow felt welcomed by the spirits of the land, the ancestors of the first Australians.

Then I awoke. I was twelve years old, at boarding school at St Peters Lutheran College in Brisbane, a young girl fresh from Papua New Guinea. Upon waking, I wondered if my dream imagery had come from a book about Aboriginal bora rings that my mother had read to me when I was little. I was comforted by the dream, as it reminded me of the colourful 'sing-sings' I had grown up with throughout my childhood in PNG. Sunshine glinted through the window and laughter pierced the air, animating the tall scribbly gum where a kookaburra was perched. The day held promise.

I asked a girl in my dorm to make my bed. I was intending to collect her laundry with mine while she did so, but I didn't articulate this. I hadn't explained my thinking; in PNG this was how everything was done. Watching my Papua New Guinean relatives and neighbours had taught me that thinking collectively and working for the group as a whole was just the way things were done. The simple sense of unity was so strong and such a given that 'please' or 'thank you' were not necessary during exchanges within my grandmother's tribe. Intuiting the needs of another, for the greater good of the tribe, was as natural as breathing. As I walked down the hallway at St Peters, I overheard my new roommate complain about me to another girl. I soon realised that to these girls I lacked manners; I was rude. I would need to say 'please' and 'thank you'. More surprising was the realisation that I would need to articulate how I would do something in return for any request I made of another. These Australian girls had no idea that we were working together, that together in the dormitory we were one! It was then that I knew I was truly in a different place.

Here on the threshold of my adolescence, I was meeting individual consciousness. Later that same day, a girl in Year Seven asked me if I had lived in a tree in my country. I wondered how someone her age could be so ignorant of PNG, Australia's closest neighbour. I was startled by the insularity of her education.

A couple of years later my Year Nine biology teacher took our class on a nature walk and showed us a pile of pipi shells left behind by Aboriginal people. I recognised it as the exact site where my corroboree dream had taken place – the hair on my skin stood tall. In PNG there is no delineation between reality and the dream world. Dreams are meant to be incorporated into this reality. Spirits were real to me, and this affirmation of my dream told me I really had been welcomed in Australia.

During my early teenage years, I mostly perceived Western individual consciousness as a selfish mindset, noticing even adults in Australia behaving without the realisation that we were all interdependent, as one. Later, however, I began to experience individual freedom. At high school I was able to select my preferred subjects of art and drama. In Australia I was able to choose my own career path. Girls in PNG often finish school in Grade Six, their focus shifting to traditional skills of gardening, child-rearing and making billums (string bags) at home. My Aunty Ku always wished she had been able to continue her schooling, like my uncles Peter and Siba had managed to do.

Years later, when I returned to PNG to launch my first book, many local women were more interested in the reason I didn't have any children. They were somewhat baffled and bemused at the purpose of a book launch. A few men tried to articulate to the gathered crowd the achievement of writing a book, but the women appeared unconvinced and whispered among themselves. For them, a book paled in comparison to a baby; it was a far greater achievement to surrender one's body to the living impulse of creation. A part of me knew the women were right.

※

In my twenties, Australia offered me the open freedom of the land. I hitchhiked with my boyfriend into the homes of generous and good-natured Australians living on land that had once been stolen from the Bundjalung, Gubbi Gubbi, Nalbo and Dallambara peoples. I recall the magic of wandering through Natural Arch at midnight with my favourite friend, Melaina, skinny-dipping in the cool water beneath a full moon. Taking a Land Rover with a mattress in the back, we slept beneath the bright desert sky, in the red centre. Once I climbed to the top and slept on the point of Mount Coonowrin, the steepest of the Glasshouse Mountains, no climbing gear, just a handsome New Zealander by my side. These were experiences that most women in PNG could never enjoy. I was aware of the opportunities granted to me as a modern Australian woman, and I savoured my adventures.

Outdoor adventures are readily available to women in Australia, a huge contrast to PNG, where it is simply not safe, smart or sensible for women to go most places alone, particularly after dark. Government-imposed curfews, barbed wire fences and outlaws with guns all contribute to a culture of fear – women in PNG fear men and the constant possibility of being raped. My Aunty May has a scar on her cheek where a *raskol* (PNG outlaw) cut her with a knife during a highway hold-up. Aunty Ku lay on the ground clutching her four-year-old boy on her stomach, fearing she was going to be raped. When I revisited PNG as an adult, six to eight relatives accompanied me wherever I went, even standing guard whenever I went to the outhouse toilet.

In PNG it was not only the women who experienced limitations. My Uncle Siba worked as a steward for Air Nuigini and frequently flew to Hawaii and Fiji. When there was trouble in his village, he had to leave his job, gather his spears and return to fight; this was a tribal expectation. Another uncle studied for four years to become an electrician, only to be told by the elders of our tribe that he would not be permitted to pursue this line of work because they did not trust white man's electricity. They had heard stories of electrocution from town folks, and their decision was final. Reluctantly, my uncle bowed to the collective fear of his village elders and gave up his career.

In Australia I learnt to balance freedom with responsibility. Education gave me a voice; it taught me to read, review and reflect. Australia afforded me my tertiary education and facilitated my degrees. I received an arts grant to help me research my book about my late Papua New Guinean grandmother. Australia delivered on its promises of opportunity. Years later, when my book won a national award, Australia affirmed its ability to help me realise my dreams. I experienced this again during my journey as the founding class teacher of Noosa Pengari Steiner School. The fledgling school epitomised hope and promise in education, and I watched the school grow from a single class of twelve children to a school offering classes from pre-prep through Year Twelve, an enriching experience in growing a community.

Australia also has a dark underbelly, and I first encountered this at my schoolies week in 1988. An attractive girlfriend accidently walked into the men's rest room at a Broadbeach venue. She was surrounded by a group of young men in their late teens, who dropped their pants and proceeded to urinate all over her. She escaped from the bathroom in tears and dashed for a taxi.

Years later, on the way out to Uluru, I pulled into a roadside cafe and asked a toothless local man what people did for entertainment in Julia Creek. He answered stoically: 'Get pissed and fight.'

'And the women?'

'Same thing.'

The problem for Australia? Julia Creek appears to be everywhere.

Women are often tough and hardened in Australia, because they have to be. Desensitisation is sometimes imperative to survival and coping, to accepting the uninspiring status quo.

In 2011 a musician friend was performing on stage in Bundaberg, the Queensland town famous for its rum. He watched a young woman get passed around from one drunken man to the next, each kissing her repeatedly and fondling her crassly before passing her on. When I heard this story, one among his large repertoire of awful pub stories, I felt a deep sadness. It was as though a greater feminine wisdom had been abandoned by both the girl and the young men. Where was their internal archetypal mother, that inner wisdom that would have allowed them to feel, to be present and awake to their intuition and essential integrity?

In the red centre, the earth around Uluru and Kata Tjuta is the colour of burnt sienna. It is as though the heart of the continent has called up the spilled, buried blood of the Indigenous men, women and children who were cruelly murdered from primal fear and human greed just 223 years ago. Wiping red dust from my eyelids for the first time, I reflected on the contrasting colours in PNG: there the earth is a deep chocolate-brown, the flora a rich emerald green, and the distant mountain ranges a violet blue, with an ethereal lilac hue. The varied colours of nature fill Papua New Guinean headdresses; it is as though the vibrant colours sing out the fact that New Guineans are citizens of an independent nation – a sharp contrast to Indigenous Australians, who remain clearly displaced on their own, blood-run-dry land.

Living in Australia, I always carried a sadness with me about colonial history. One day I witnessed a rare sight: an Indigenous Australian man in Noosa. He was quietly handing out flyers when a police car pulled up and two cops escorted him away. I wondered if a black man's presence in predominantly white Noosa was simply not acceptable in 1997? I recalled how in the 1980s it was socially acceptable to feature a black man on the popular TV show *Neighbours*, but only if he had a British accent. Evidently, it was deemed too risky to celebrate an Aussie blackfella on the show.

During my twenty-nine years in Australia, I experienced one truth: modern, mainstream Australia lacks a guiding archetypal feminine wisdom – the willingness to behold that which is ugly, dark or unpalatable with a sense of empathy that leads to acceptance and transformation. After the Dreamtime, no goddess, representing balance, has ever been revered in Australia. This manifests in the imbalance of the masculine. We find men getting pissed in pubs, swallowing their un-cried tears and looking for fights to express their frustration, right across the nation. Meanwhile our millions of cars and trucks continually run over a million Aboriginal women's songlines in utter ignorance.

Listening to the common, day-to-day speech of Australians we encounter an abundance of clipped vowels and harsh consonants. Expressions are short and sharp, often lacking melody. Growing up in PNG taught me that feelings are captured in vowel sounds. It was common to hear New Guineans sing out 'Aiiee!' or 'Aaiio!' to express any emotions, from fear to joy to sadness, with loudly exclaimed, expansive vowel sounds. Free emotional expression is common in PNG, where people often cry and wail in public; it is an accepted, even expected, part of daily life. In Australia vowel sounds are tightly clipped and emotional dialogue is often tight-lipped. Maxims like 'she'll be right', or 'no worries, mate' ensure that true-blue Aussies are not allowed to explore or express feelings. These common colloquialisms deny individuals their right to an emotional literacy, to become intimate with fear, loss, pain and regret.

In Australia I often refrained from expressing my emotions fully in public. I learnt to articulate my feelings, which was socially acceptable, but I wasn't free to feel them. There were times when I wanted to cry and even wail aloud, yet the social codes of repression were too different from PNG's. I was most negatively affected when I was in a situation where I experienced truth in its fullness being denied. For example, when I learnt that former colleagues were having an affair, using my home as a venue for their extramarital liaisons, I felt deeply hurt by their collusion, and sad for their spouses and families. When I was with their children, whom I was teaching, I wanted to cry. I learnt from watching those around me that in Australia it was often more appropriate to judge than feel.

When I learnt that my mother-in-law did not have the courage or compassion to tell my husband the true identity of his biological father, I felt deeply sad. My husband did not allow himself to feel or cry in front of me, and I felt I was not allowed to express my grief. I watched those around me adopt positive affirmations, rather than feel and express true emotion.

As I remained hidden in my early corroboree dream, a part of me also had to remain hidden during my years in Australia. A part of my femininity found no safe place to emerge within the mainstream infrastructure, or even in most day-to-day dialogue and interactions. This hidden part of myself could only appear briefly in the solitude of nature, at folk festivals, yoga retreats and among a few close friends.

I have recently left Australia with deep gratitude for the memories and the worthy gifts of freedom, opportunity and choice it gave me. I moved to Indonesia with the hope of encountering some of the aspects I found missing in Australia: a clearer emotional literacy, better attunement to the earth and natural cycles, and more frequent honouring of our collective humanity, through open smiles and daily exchanges of human integrity.

Having enjoyed the freedom to think and do in Australia, I am now ready to embrace the heart of another culture – one that honours feeling – to return to my own feminine balance.

ADIB KHAN
Here, There

'*Practices of displacement might emerge as constitutive of cultural meanings rather than as their simple transfer or extension.*' – James Clifford

The full significance of place polygamy did not occur to me until I paid a second visit to my country of origin, Bangladesh, in the late 1990s. Since then, I have wondered about a sense of loss that has sporadically manifested itself in different ways and sometimes at unexpected moments. Such intimations of privation contradict the success of assimilation, underpinned by understanding, acceptance and willing participation, in the mainstream culture of my adopted land.

On my initial return visit to Bangladesh in 1983, I was not troubled by my choice to settle in Australia. Since then a further broadening of cultural perspectives has generated dissatisfaction. I want to recapture what there was and keep what I now have. I live in Australia for reasons that range from the superficial and banal to the aesthetic and the socio-political dimensions of this deceptively complex culture. I enjoy the laid-back lifestyle, the beaches in summer, the mystical spatiality of the outback, the variety of the landscape, the diversity of its cultures and the egalitarianism of a population that has little tolerance for class structures and snobbery.

Australia is not without flaws. The 'children overboard' affair still rankles me. I cringe with embarrassment when overseas visitors mention Pauline Hanson, and I wish more could be done for the homeless people in our community. There are aspects of inequality and corruption within the infrastructure, some of our politicians are often insular and lack altruism, and we could be more proactive about global concerns such as climate change and refugees. This is, however, an open society where contentious issues are freely argued, often with great animation, without fear of repercussion. There is communal pride in living here and an infectious enthusiasm for enjoying what the country has to offer.

Adapting to life in Australia has not posed any notable difficulties for me. Perhaps the main reason for fitting easily into the mainstream culture here was that language did not create any barrier, although I quickly discovered that colloquial Australian English had its own distinct identity and nuances that could lead to misunderstandings. I vividly remember my arrival at Tullamarine airport in March 1973. I meekly walked through customs and immigration and headed for a kiosk where I ordered a cup of coffee. 'Black or white?' the peroxide blonde behind the counter asked. Warning bells sounded immediately. I recalled the cautionary advice that I had received at the

Australian High Commission in Dhaka, about possible pockets of racism in the country. I looked at the woman serving me and decided not to make an issue out of what I thought was unnecessary provocation – I was too jaded and tired to get into a slinging match. 'White,' I replied tonelessly. Imagine my surprise and embarrassment when she poured milk into the polystyrene cup and handed it to me. It was a defining moment. From then on, I became extremely cautious about accusing others of prejudice without examining my own perceptions and perspectives of situations and people.

My connection with Melbourne has always been special. The city pulsates with a beat that synchronises with my own rhythm of living. I came as a student to Monash University during the Whitlam era when accommodation, food and transportation were cheap and the life of a foreign tertiary student was nowhere near as much of a struggle as it can be today. Those were the days when one could go out looking for a part-time job in a milk bar, a petrol station, a restaurant or a bar and find employment within a few days. Of course, in the 1970s, Melbourne was not as culturally diverse or sophisticated a city as it is today.

Even though I eventually moved to Ballarat to teach, I never lost my affinity with Melbourne. Now I am fortunate enough to be able to divide my time between both places, enjoying the calmness and easy pace of country living without losing touch with the excitement of the city. In Ballarat, I write, read, garden and grow vegetables. When boredom begins to creep in, I shift my base to Richmond.

The astonishing culinary diversity, the concerts and theatre, the galleries and the art movies in Melbourne are all there to enjoy for the entire year. It is a city that opens itself to curiosity and leisurely exploration. One has to go looking in the not-so-well-known suburbs, streets and lanes to find quaint places and oddities that delight and surprise. I immerse myself in the city's culture without inhibition and at the expense of being labelled a hedonist. In winter I can walk to the Melbourne Cricket Ground to watch Hawthorn battle it out with any of the other Australian Football League teams and get stuck into the opposition and the umpires without a modicum of objectivity. Years ago, a friend lectured me against the notion of quiet enjoyment at the footy. He said something to the effect that as a Hawthorn supporter I had to be firmly biased towards the players and the club. All umpiring decisions against Hawthorn were wrong, our players never fouled and when we lost, an international conspiracy had prevailed. Such a mind-set, my friend concluded, was a cultural imperative. I have learnt to tolerate commercially baked pies, slathered with tomato sauce, and I leave the ground elated or else full of gripe about the vagaries of fate. In the summer months, it is time for test cricket, that giddily wonderful ritual of tradition, brain and brawn, and perhaps a peek-in at the Australian Open.

Yes! It is a good life.

Yet, there is this other side of me, prodded by memory, that periodically broods and yearns for a lost world that was once mine. If, as the expatriate British writer Lawrence Durrell contended, 'human beings are expressions of their landscapes', then the landscape of my past is stubbornly entrenched in my psyche, its voices and configurations undiminished by the intervening years since I left my native land.

Bangladesh is not a place of any great affluence or blessed with many natural resources. The country has irrevocably changed. Dhaka, the capital where I grew up, is no longer the sleepy city of a few million people. It is now an uncontrollable metropolis of nearly thirteen million people, impossibly crowded, polluted and chaotic. As soon as I arrived there on my second visit back after moving to Australia, I became impatient to leave. During the three weeks of my stay, I was in a continual state of denial about my confused sense of belonging. The extent to which I had been westernised in the years of my absence was a jarring reality check. The cacophony of incessant noises made a mockery of my craving for order and silence. The colours and the smells overwhelmed me. Walking the streets among throngs of jostling people was an intimidating experience. I struggled with traffic chaos and pollution. I was no longer used to this kind of panoramic exposure to life in all its facets.

I realised that I guarded my privacy with the utmost vigil. I expected everyone to meet my standard of punctuality and was uncomfortable with the steady stream of relatives who came to see me. It was also the month of Ramadan. Although there was no compulsion for me to fast, the practice of feasting at irregular hours was a source of unease and wonderment. Life here was disorderly. I never adjusted to the screeching siren that woke everyone for *sehri*, the custom of eating before dawn as a prelude to the day's fasting. The noise, the aroma of freshly prepared food, the banter, the laughter and the call for prayers were disconcerting, to say the least. Yet, there was something endearing in this spontaneous and joyous response to an established custom from which I felt excluded. I began to envy the communal togetherness. Once, I was an integral part of this familial activity.

The feast of Eid marked the end of the holy month. The morning's mandatory visit to the mosque for prayers began with an elaborate breakfast that included the traditional *shemoi*, a sweet made from vermicelli. For several days, I had been dreading the event. Much to the silent disapproval of family members, I went out of my way to announce that I was no longer a practising Muslim. No, I was not a *nastik* (atheist) and neither was I an agnostic. I was a zetetic, I pronounced. There were puzzled looks and a whispered question. 'What is a zetetic?' a cousin asked. I smiled and gave the most convoluted of answers that could be imagined. There was safety in confusion, I thought rather smugly. No one would dare to ask me to go to the mosque in case I behaved like an ignorant foreigner – who was also a zetetic! – destined to embarrass the family.

The morning of Eid did not begin promisingly. There was a knock on my bedroom door and a servant informed me that it was my turn for a morning bath. A shower or a bath...well, either was okay. Another knock and this time it was one of my cousins wishing me Eid Mubarak and handing me a skull cap and a new set of white clothes: a loose-fitting pair of cotton trousers, a singlet and a thin, long shirt known as *panjabi*. After breakfast, the men and boys gathered on the veranda. I was repeatedly invited to join them. It seemed that all my good work about the dodgy state of zeteticism had been in vain.

I turned to a favourite aunt and said weakly, 'I don't think it's such a good idea for me to go to the mosque.'

She handed me a prayer mat, smiling blandly, as if she did not understand, and nudged me gently in the direction of the men. So off we went, members of the Khan clan, resplendently dressed in white, like a cricket team going out to field.

The mosque was crowded and we had to lay our mats on the road outside. The muezzin's call to prayer sounded to me like an incantation intended to evoke a past where, as a child, I fervently believed in all that was supposedly significant about Eid. For a moment there was an impossible wish to eradicate rational thinking and scepticism, peel back the years and be where I once was, blessed with a raw imagination and outrageous dreams of an opulent afterlife.

The prayers began and the entire congregation was

on its knees, bending to touch the ground with our foreheads in submission to Allah. The silence was broken by the sound of my knees creaking loudly like rusty hinges. It was agony sitting on a hard surface with my legs tucked under me. A cousin sat next to me. From the corner of my eyes, I followed his movements. My fists rested on top of my knees. He uncurled the index finger of his right hand and raised it in the air to indicate that there is only one God. I did the same. Then I turned my head to the right to greet the angel on my shoulder. I did the same on the other side, except this time there was a sharp click, followed by a shooting pain. Maybe a stiff neck was a light punishment meted out by the ethereal, winged beings for my religious profligacy.

The prayers finally ended and I felt as if I had been put through a meat grinder. The men rose to their feet and greeted each other. I was embraced by strangers who murmured, 'Eid Mubarak!' This was a suburban mosque and most people knew each other. What struck me was the lack of reservation about strangers. No questions were asked and I was not ignored. The community spirit was strong – I was drawn into its mesh. My relatives introduced me to their friends and acquaintances. We discussed politics and global affairs. I was invited for afternoon tea by people I had just met. I was no longer afraid that I was an intrusive alien. The rest of the day was to be taken up by visitations and the culmination of the festival turned out to be a grand and noisy feast in the company of my family members and their close friends.

In the middle of the banquet, memory tunnelled me back to a time when I had never questioned my place in a community, simply because I knew no other. I suddenly thought of the return trip to Australia. A sharp current of panic rippled through me... There was regret and yearning for a lost communal life. For the first time I acknowledged the shortcomings of place polygamy and felt the loneliness of living in that narrow stretch of No Man's Land, able to participate in the activities of polarised cultures but unable to belong to either.

I returned to Australia with a blurred vision of what the future held for me and burdened with the certainty that the individual living in diaspora is a divided self, destined to experience perpetual tension between the empirical reality of a current location and the remembrance of what once was in a distant land.

The idea of culture, both from the perspective of academic discourse and a layperson's point of view, is expansive and inclusive of such a vast array of topics that an attempt to find a reductive and singularly comprehensive definition would fail. Yet it is too important a concept to bypass simply because of the degree of difficulty of interpretation or definition. The word 'culture' not only mutates in meaning and implications with the passage of time, but it also embodies human evolution in its entire gamut of development and change. Personalities are shaped by cultural factors that encompass ideologies, beliefs, attitudes and aesthetics. Ultimately, values are determined by their influences. The anthropologist

Clifford Geertz claimed that 'there is no such thing as a human nature independent of culture'. In other words, both communally and individually, culture shapes us in its web of socio-politics, religion and rituals, and economy, linking our past with our present condition.

The impression of culture on an individual is complicated enough, but its impact is even more intricate when one considers the effects of different cultures, both indigenous and adopted, in the diasporic experience. For instance, I now prioritise the significance of individuality as a fundamental right of every citizen. At the same time, I am aware of the barrenness of solitariness and the possible effects of loneliness. The potential for selfishness and greed is an ever-present danger. There is no better example of the damage it can cause than the recent financial crisis that has plagued so many democratic societies. I advocate the benefits of a nuclear family but I have vivid memories of the advantages of an extended family. Whenever I exasperated my mother to the point that a smack was in the offing, there was always an aunt or a cousin to whisk me away until my mother had calmed down. Family members were often buffers against the possible repercussions of anger.

As William Safran suggested, members of a diasporic community have tenacious memories about their homeland with which they continue to 'relate, personally or vicariously…in one way or another, and their ethnocommunal consciousness and solidarity are importantly defined by the existence of such a relationship'. The relationship, however, is fraught with frustration because of its elusiveness. It is a connection with recalled voices, images of people and events in specific locations that no longer exist tangibly in the ways that they are remembered as the fabric of a past life.

The passing years have led me to confront and accept the consequences of dispersal. There has been a gradual understanding of fragmentation as part of a blueprint of a dualistic life. It is a scheme that demands an imaginative link with the past to understand the present. That imaginative link, for me, is creating fiction that enables me to reconfigure the past and scrutinise it to locate the coordinates of who and what I am. It has not, however, resolved the conflicts that have arisen from the experience of cultural diversity. Age has also taught me to arbitrate and attempt to seek reconciliation between the fractured halves that constitute a migrant's dilemma. I have to live with the knowledge that I will never be entirely successful in my attempts. There are separate lives to be led: one in memory and the other in the physical reality of the present. I no longer allow my inherited subcontinental values about family and community to clash with Western desirability for freedom and individuality and create mayhem. I am like a parent who sends his fighting twin children to separate rooms to help cool things down, though that does not alleviate self-doubt about where things might have gone wrong.

Whatever the nature and intensity of the struggle, I try to contain it within myself in an arena where, in Salman Rushdie's words, 'I buck, I snort, I whinny, I rear, I kick.' But I continue to live behind a benign mask of contentment. At times I wish that I could erase memory, at others I nourish and encourage what it offers. I am both here and there. Like Rushdie, I remain undecided about the way my life has shaped itself and prefer not to make a definitive choice about where I should be.

To return to Bangladesh would mean another massive dislocation and cultural readjustment. I am no longer a resilient young man seeking new frontiers. Above everything else, it would mean distancing myself from my children – who were born in Australia and grew up here – and even possible estrangement from them. Staying in Australia will continue to niggle me as I grow older. One's ending should ideally be where one began. It is a fitting completion of the cycle of living. The uncertainty of what might be the right decision creates anguish, but I have to live with it. That is the payment for the knowledge and the rich experiences I have gained from 'living' simultaneously in two places.

ALI ALIZADEH
Sally

I didn't know how to talk to her. I didn't know the exact words, or the correct pronunciation of these words, to communicate what I wanted to say to her. English was my second language, but she and my feelings for her went beyond words. I didn't want to remain distant from her, or from what it was that she signified for me. I didn't want to be an unloved foreigner forever.

Sally was more reserved than most other kids in school, but she was by no means as shy as me. She was a petite and rather frail creature. She had a couple of friends with whom she ate lunch, and unlike me she did not spend her time at school in a state of perpetual trepidation. She was in my Visual Arts class and seemed like a generally well-adjusted teenage girl, although she was not as cheerful and strident as many other Year Twelve girls. I felt that she was something of a loner, or perhaps a dreamer – a bit like me, or so I liked to think. And I was sure that she didn't have a boyfriend.

Not that Sally had shown any interest in me. She had simply been going about her business, without saying a word to me, for as long as I'd been aware of her. She was, as far as I'd come to fantasise about her, a normal schoolgirl the same age as me. I'd never heard her spoken of as a 'slut' — or really spoken of at all — around school. Although by now I was spending most of my time avoiding other kids — especially the 'footy crowd', who terrorised me whenever I was in their proximity — I was still aware of what the boys said, often boisterously, about most girls. I knew about their exploits at parties that I wasn't invited to, and I was glad to never hear Sally's name mentioned amid the footy-heads' triumphant claims of receiving blowjobs in darkened backyards and filthy bedrooms.

I came to believe that Sally was a class apart, far more cultivated than others at our vulgar, xenophobic high school. And even more whimsically, I thought that, unlike others, she didn't find me a fat, thickly accented laughing-stock.

But I didn't know how to approach her.

By now I had lost confidence in my ability to hold anything like a conversation with anyone. Despite my success in picking up basic conversational English rather quickly in Lismore upon arriving in Australia two years earlier, my experiences of being constantly misunderstood by teachers and laughed at by my classmates in Brisbane had left me deeply anxious about both my accent and my command of the language. My parents spoke Farsi at home, and there was hardly anyone at school with whom I could practice my spoken English.

Yet I had come to convince myself, perhaps

subconsciously, that Sally and I were destined to be together.

I thought about Sally every time my mother moaned that we had migrated to Australia so that I wouldn't be conscripted into the Islamic Republic's army as a child soldier, and that therefore it was my fault that her life had been ruined. And I thought about Sally's soft blue eyes every time my unemployed father shouted at me (in Farsi, of course) due to my not being sufficiently deferential towards him. And it was Sally's sandy curls I thought about when the footy-heads howled joyfully, 'Ali! Say something! Speak English!' every time I happened to be anywhere near them in the school grounds.

So I had to let Sally know that I was in love with her. With my chubby cheeks, dark skin and thick monobrow, I could hardly have expected to remind her of any of the heartthrobs of the era's popular culture – ie the athletic and uniformly Anglo-Germano-Celtic stars of *Beverly Hills, 90210* – but I was blindly optimistic that a girl as wonderful as Sally would not be into these nefarious teen idols, or the local 'hunks' who modelled themselves after them. I felt that there was a reasonable chance she might not find me entirely repulsive.

However, I didn't know how to communicate my yearning to her; that is, not until I convinced my parents to let me go and see the new French movie *Cyrano de Bergerac*. I'd been more or less obsessed with all things French since my childhood in Iran, and was thrilled when my parents gave me enough money (a considerable sum for a family of unemployed migrants living on welfare) to go and see the subtitled movie at an art-house cinema in the city, albeit accompanied by my father. I was immediately inspired by the story of an ugly soldier who seduces a beautiful noblewoman with his poetry – but with, alas, tragic consequences; it occurred to me that perhaps I too could express myself to my divine Sally, if not verbally, then in writing.

A few days later, as I was sitting – or, more accurately, hiding – behind the library building to eat my lunch, I saw the lanky figure of a boy with whom I had exchanged a few words in our Ancient History class. To my alarm, I noticed that he was on his way towards me.

Andrew had never been openly friendly, but I couldn't remember him joining the others in laughing at me. I continued to chew my apple as he sat next to me and wiped blood off his nose. He didn't wait for me to acknowledge his presence before telling me hastily, and hatefully, about the fight he'd just been in. It turned out that Andrew was my fellow victim in the school's oppressive hierarchy: due to being no good at sport, he too was a member of the underclass, of those abused and intimidated by the footy crowd.

'Someone's gonna teach them cunts a lesson. I'll fuckin' blow their heads off, eh. My dad's got a gun.'

I didn't know if I should believe him or if he was simply letting off steam. So I decided to do what I was good at: remain silent and keep my thoughts to myself.

'Why the fuck don't you ever stick up for yourself,

man? I'll help you. My brother's a tough son of a bitch, eh.'

He was now staring at me with a disconcerting intensity while dabbing his nose with a piece of toilet paper. I had to say something.

'What was the fight over?'

'That bitch Samantha was all over me at Dan's party. And then fuckin' Joel says to me he fucked her last weekend and she's, like, a dirty bitch and shit. So I go to Samantha to see if she's really fucked Joel and she says she hasn't, so I tell Joel he's a lying piece of shit and the next thing you know all his footy mates are there and – fuckin' cunts – they just came up behind me, eh... And the next thing I see is Samantha, right, egging Joel and them on, and she's getting all excited watching them gang up on me. Stupid bitch. They're all a bunch of stupid fuckin' bitches. All the chicks in this school are stupid ugly scrags, eh.'

I should've kept my mouth shut, but this was perhaps one of the very few times I had been engaged in a conversation for a very long time; besides, there was something I needed to get off my own chest.

'Not all of them. Some girl here is very nice.'

Andrew's frown flipped into a smirk without losing any of its intensity.

'Yeah? Who've you got the hots for? C'mon man, I won't tell anyone. I promise.'

'Sal – no one. I'm not interested in girls here.'

'Sally Thompson?! No shit! Really? You like that ugly cow?'

I sealed my lips, knowing that I had said too much already.

'Sorry, man, just teasing you. She's really hot, eh. Honest. She's a real babe. Have you asked her out? She's single. You should ask her out. Go on.'

I didn't have to say anything for Andrew to understand that a fat, pimply guy as shy, socially awkward and linguistically challenged as me didn't have it in him to just walk up to 'a real babe' and ask her out on a date.

'I'll ask her out for you, eh. You want me to do that? She's in my next class. She's got nice tits.'

'I will…phone-call her.'

'But you haven't got her phone number, have you? Look, why don't you just write her a letter or something? I know where she lives. I'll drop it off at her place. Promise.'

On the day I wrote my letter to Sally, I had been yet again bullied by the footy-heads and told to 'go back to where ya came from'; I had been yet again disheartened by my teachers' unwillingness to prevent or stop the bullies from tormenting me; I had been yet again yelled at by my father upon entering our small apartment for not seeming sufficiently happy and grateful to be greeted by him; and had been yet again told by my mother that she hated Australia with all her heart.

In other words, it was just another day in my seventeen-year-old adolescent's life when I sat down at the desk in my bedroom to write, using my very best vocabulary and syntax, the letter to Sally. How many drafts did I write? I must have checked my spelling against a dictionary. I remember enough of the letter's content to reconstruct it as follows:

Hi Sally,

I'm sorry that I am writing to you instead of talking to you. I think you are very beautiful and I'm very shy around people. I like to talk to you and ask you to go and see a movie with me. Do you like Europeans films? There's a great movie about a poet who loves a girl but he's very ugly and he's scared of being rejected by her. So he writes poems for her. Do you like poems? I really like your collage painting that you did for the first assignment this year. I like your eyes. And I really like the way you laugh when something funny happens in class. You have a very soft beautiful smile. And I like it that you don't laugh at me when someone makes fun of my accent. I really want to talk to you. We can go and see a Hollywood film if you prefer. Most Hollywood films are stupid and boring. And I don't like dumb things and dumb people. That's why I like you. You're very smart and beautiful. I wish I had your phone number. Can I call you? My phone number is…

And so on. I actually did draft the letter a number of times, and the final version was inscribed in my very best cursive handwriting, on special beige letter-writing paper. I placed it in a plain (but, in my view, stylish) envelope before giving it to my one and only friend Andrew, who had promised to deposit it in my beloved's letterbox after school on Friday.

Despite the relative backwardness of early 1990s communication technologies, my supplication went viral, spreading almost as fast as any future internet virus.

I arrived at school the following Monday morning apprehensive at not having received a phone call from the letter's cherished addressee over the weekend. As I crossed the school oval, I was greeted by a larger-than-usual throng of overexcited bullies, now including my grinning messenger Andrew – who had, yes, made sure that everyone in school saw my earnest words of hope and devotion before delivering them to Sally.

'Ya fuckin' creep', 'Ya fuckin' loser', '*I love you Sally! You're smart and beautiful!*' and so on, they jeered at me; I didn't know what to do. Best to do what I normally did: keep silent and avoid my tormentors. I started to walk past the bullies, towards the relative safety of the dismal faux amphitheatre where our morning assemblies were held, but an empty can of soft drink flew from the footy crowd and hit me on the chest. One of the footy-heads growled 'Fuck off home, ya fuckin' loser.' My chest hurt, but I continued to walk. When another outcast (a gay male student) had run away from a pack of bullies one lunchtime earlier in the year, he had been chased, cornered and badly beaten.

I didn't see Sally at school that day. When she did finally call me that evening, my mother made sure to stay in the room where the phone was, perhaps to overhear the all-too-brief and anticlimactic exchange between her innocent teenage son and the potentially indecent young Western temptress at the other end of the line.

'Look, I'm not interested. I don't want to go out with you. I hardly know you. Stop coming around to my house and dropping weird stuff in our letterbox – my dad will call the police. Okay?' With my mother watching me closely as I held the handset and listened to Sally's curt rejection, I couldn't allow myself to get emotional and remonstrate. I only mumbled, 'Okay. I'm sorry. So sorry.'

I hung up the phone and choked back tears. My mother said something but I couldn't bring myself to be around her or anyone else. I needed to be alone. I ignored her and trudged to my room. I could hear my father shouting after me: '*Pesar-e beesharaf, chera javaab-e so'al-e maadarat-o nemeedi?*' (Literally: 'Dishonourable boy [perhaps best translated as 'Son of a bitch'], why won't you answer your mother's question?')

But for once I wasn't scared of my father's threatening voice.

Nothing he was capable of could possibly match what I had just experienced. I was feeling so miserable that my mother's melodramatic display of homesickness later that evening failed to make me feel any worse. I felt so shattered that even putting up with the rabid schoolkids and enduring the odiously indifferent teachers for the rest of Year Twelve seemed like a minor hardship. I felt that no one in Australia would ever accept me now that even the angelic Sally had turned me down. It was now clear to me that Sally was but the first of the women who would reject me in the years to come; faced with a future of utter loneliness, my present-day trials seemed childish and insignificant.

Did the experience make me dislike Australia and Australians? Did my being an immigrant, struggling with the language and not looking like the other kids add a uniquely dismal dimension to an otherwise universal experience of unrequited love? Perhaps. But what I'm sure of is that after my encounter with Sally – if it can be called that – I felt that I had very little left to lose. I felt that the worst thing imaginable had happened, and that things couldn't get any worse. And so, life started to seem a little less grim.

LILY YULIANTI FARID

The Range Hood and the Grease

Living in Melbourne as a foreigner always drives my mind to imagine someone else's kitchen. The TV shows such as *MasterChef* and *My Kitchen Rules* remind me of the concept of the 'dry kitchen' introduced by my mother when I was a little girl. In 1984, my mother built two kitchens in our house in my hometown of Makassar – the dry kitchen and the wet.

Our dry kitchen served as a display in the corner of our dining room, hardly ever used. 'Western people have a kitchen like this', an interior designer explained to my mother. Cupboards hung on the walls, filled with collectable items – plates and cups used only for special occasions. The stove and the oven were clean, shiny. Not for daily use. Their design was sleek and modern.

The wet kitchen was the centre of meal production, where our maids – yes, it's typically middle-class in Asian countries to have one or two maids in the house – prepared food for my whole family, day and night. The maids worked barefoot on the wet kitchen floor. There was a gas stove, cooking pots, and tins filled with spices and herbs; fresh and dried chillies dangled from the kitchen wall and black stains marked the ceiling. Sometimes we found cockroaches and rats that had run into the kitchen's corners. The wet kitchen is the *real* kitchen in most Indonesian households.

It didn't take long for me to spot the differences between Australian and Indonesian kitchens. After arriving in Melbourne as an international student, I spent my first days finding accommodation. House inspections became a routine agenda. I visited houses and flats, and saw various displays of dry kitchens just like the one we had in Makassar. In one single-bedroom flat, a small kitchen was located right in front of the door. In a two-bedroom unit, a kitchen was attached to the living room? I tried quickly to absorb all the information supplied by rental agents chaperoning me around: did I want an open-plan kitchen or a separate dining room, a gas or an electric stove, a range hood or an exhaust fan? These Western kitchens offered a different kind of culture shock for me.

Kitchen in the living room?

Wait a minute…no one would build a house with this kind of layout, I thought, using my grandmother's words: 'It's a taboo!'

For many Indonesians, the kitchen should be placed at the back of the house for this reason: it is the centre of meal production for the family and is considered a wet, chaotic and busy space; therefore it must be hidden from visitors' sightlines. Instead of using the terms 'dry' or 'wet' kitchen as my mother did, some of our relatives referred to the wet kitchen as the 'dirty kitchen', describing it as smoky and smelly. It is stacked with cooking pots, and herbs and dried spices dangle on the walls...and on floors.

I grew up with a sense that a kitchen *should* be separated from the other rooms of a house, as it symbolises social structures and hierarchical relationships among Indonesian families. It's a cultural given. Maids, in many cases, are allowed only in the kitchen and dining areas – their designated areas. In a strongly patriarchal society, where the husband is the breadwinner for the family, it's traditionally understood that he should *not* enter the kitchen. Cooking and food preparation are considered a female domain. My father never entered our kitchen.

I burst into laughter now when I imagine having both my father and grandmother in an open-plan Melbourne kitchen. How would my father avoid the kitchen that's installed right behind the front door? My conservative grandmother, may she rest in peace, would kick my father out of the house, saying: 'It's taboo to have a man in the kitchen!' In Melbourne, both my husband and son help me a great deal in the kitchen. They adore cooking. This is unusual for men and boys in my extended family back in Makassar.

Remembering my childhood, it dawned on me that there was something missing in my mother's modern, display-only Western kitchen in Makassar: a range hood. My eyes always stuck on the range hood when I inspected a house or apartment to live in. Its shape and sounds – noisy!

In our wet Makassar kitchen, various columns of smoke from hours, days and weeks of meals climb the kitchen walls and fly through ventilation louvres, spreading the familiar smells of fragrant rice, baked fish and stir-fried vegetables. The strong, recognisable smells can reach our neighbours' homes. In my Western-style Melbourne kitchen, the range hood, with its noisy sound, magically exhausts all smells and tries its best to remove smoke, grease and oils from accumulating where they should. 'Stay clean!' it says. 'Never spread smoke and smells to your neighbour!'

Makassar: thousands of miles from Australia is my mother's wet kitchen, its stained walls full of memories and the history of our family's food production.

Melbourne: the dry and clean kitchen, looking sleek yet lifeless in the open-plan lounge. What should I prepare here? A simple sandwich of canned tuna and no cause to emit smell or smoke? A bowl of salad and bread like other Australians I've met?

When I finally got my first one-bedroom flat in the Melbourne suburb of West Brunswick back in 2001, I spent hours in front of the stove – turning on the range hood, then off again, listening to its whirring and recalling memories. It's a remedy for displacement.

'Once you have established yourself here, in your own house, during your study, you will feel the loneliness,' a friend who had arrived in Australia earlier once told me. She was totally right. I did get served the homesick course just after I moved in to my new place. I found myself sitting in the kitchen, operating the range hood, my mind walking through my childhood. On again, then off. On. Off. On...*whirrr.*

During these moments I often asked myself, what if grandmother and mother had installed range hoods in their kitchens? There would have been no black stains on the ceilings above each of their stoves. They would have had better, cleaner and safer kitchens, I thought. But wait! I challenged my own thoughts. Indonesian kitchens would *always* be like the wet kitchen we had in our home in Makassar. We love those wet-kitchen floors and we think nothing of – or to put it more precisely, our maids think nothing of – putting all of our dirty plates on the floor, getting a bucket full of water, then squatting to wash them.

As a child, I sat next to my mother on our kitchen floor at the end of Ramadan. Accompanied by our maids, each year we spent hours cooking special dishes from dawn to dusk and deeper into the night. We often made my mother's special dishes: chicken with galangal and coconut milk, steamed rice with coconut milk wrapped in banana leaves, spicy stir-fried beef. Smells of these dishes reached the front yards of our neighbours' homes, as the scents from their efforts did to ours. My mother's special dishes were cooked for at least six hours and I can still imagine how smoky our kitchen was during, how the smoke settled into our eyes and brewed tears of happiness.

Perhaps we Indonesians allow – *need* – smoke from our stoves to drift up to our kitchen ceilings and remain there forever, marking the story of all the dishes we have prepared. In remembering my childhood on that Makassar kitchen floor from afar, I play with my own imagination: what if I installed a range hood in my mother's kitchen? Another version of me appears in my thoughts to challenge the idea: 'No, no! Don't do that! Our wet kitchens have their own style and standards. A range hood would suck out all memories and make our kitchen walls spotless, history-less. Lifeless.'

A kitchen is the only place where I can strongly smell the memories of my grandmother, my mother and all of my family members back in Indonesia. Occasionally, I even take out my mortar and pestle just to have a play, to feel the sound of my mother's kitchen in Makassar or my grandmother's kitchen in Soppeng.

I have moved to an unfamiliar place and try to fill up my modern kitchen drawers with my mother's spices and herbs. I stock cloves, turmeric, tamarind, galangal, lemongrass and canned coconut milk in an attempt to resemble the kitchen of my childhood. A kitchen has been the only place where I can summon my memories after eating a sandwich or meat pie, as I do during my days at the University of Melbourne.

I imagine many other migrants would have a similar story when arriving on foreign soil. People migrate to a new place, carrying with them a kitchen drawer full of herbs, spices and recipes from their motherland packed into their minds and hearts. I brought palm sugars and locally produced tea that my mother bought specially from a village market. I took notes on her signature dishes – prawn red curry, fish-head tamarind soup and palm-sugar pudding – and their preparation, with a special footnote that Mother's treasured recipes require fresh coconut milk from a market (as she always warns me).

'Did you have a chance to try the recipes there?' my mother asked me once in a telephone conversation.

'I've cooked prawn chilli curry and tamarind fish-head soup, just like yours,' I answered.

'And how did you get fresh coconut milk there?'

'I use canned coconut milk.'

'Oh, *my* recipe requires fresh coconut milk,' mother complained.

In my cooking experiments, I have settled on (and prefer) using fresh skinny cow's milk instead of canned coconut milk – my mother sounded unhappy with that decision when I first told her.

'Well, if you can't find the fresh one, canned coconut milk will do, but not cow's milk!' mother persisted.

I patiently explained that Australia is a multicultural country. In Melbourne, there are plenty of Indonesian,

Malaysian, Vietnamese, Thai and Chinese restaurants. Asian groceries have mushroomed in the city centre and inner as well as outer suburbs in recent years. Giant supermarkets have Asian food aisles. I told her that it is much easier now to find coconut milk, but replacing it with cow's milk is a health-related issue.

One precious lesson I have learnt, I told my mother, is to consume healthier foods here in Australia while remaining vigilant in my search for delicious dishes that my Indonesian tongue and stomach crave. Replacing coconut milk with fresh milk (or sometimes with plain light yoghurt) was a small step I took for reasons of health and practicality. My mother tells me how Makassar has been growing into a modern city, with more food courts and restaurants serving Western foods. She tells me that every time she is invited to dine out with my brothers' families, my nephews order pizza, steak and chicken burgers. Are these new layers of smoke collecting on my family history?

In my small flat in Melbourne, I have watched myself transform into an amateur cook in search of my childhood dishes. I cook Asian dishes and have realised how I still heavily rely on homemade-style foods like the ones I had in Makassar. Rice is still my staple food. Not bread.

I once went to an Asian grocer with a mission – to find frozen banana leaves. My goal was to make traditional steamed rice with coconut milk wrapped in banana leaves called *burasa*. The process was more complicated than I remembered it being, requiring skilled and nimble fingers to fold the leaves neat and tidy. No pot, pan, counter or floor space seemed right for the job. After five hours, I had to admit that my mission had failed. Discouraged, I called my mother and told her how difficult it was…and it was then that I realised how simple dishes from my childhood have become something un-doable here in my tiny Melbourne kitchen. It's a painful feeling.

I have built a special relationship with kitchens, their many incarnations and variations, and I have driven myself closer to each little thing in my current one – every spice, recipe, saucepan and button on my range hood – as this is the only place I have the authority to recreate my hometown.

As a writer, I find ways to observe someone's life from the details of their kitchen. When I visit a new friend's house – friends who are new to Australia, like me – I cannot keep myself from looking at their range hood, jutting out from a tiny cooking space.

My eyes trace the streaks of yellowed grease down to where they pool in the corners of a stainless-steel filter panel, reminding myself of Indonesian kitchens. Here too, I know there is a story – perhaps a history – of their longings of home left behind in the grease.

JUAN GARRIDO-SALGADO

'I Have Three Wounds': Of Life, Love and Death

TERREMOTO

All of what remained in us was down to hours – daily, weekly accumulations of them – silent spans like we were puppets without any public function. My family and I were silenced humans, wounds of exile struggling to enjoy just a moment in an empty Adelaide street.

Arriving in Australia was like going to a previously undiscovered desert in our family's soul; our words and smiles became irrelevant, our tears and sorrows the only sense of life. My young children, Tania and Lenin, seemed as if they were two ancient characters from Dostoyevsky's *Crime and Punishment*. Not knowing any English, we got lost in the solitude of this unknown land and, clinging together, would come to be people destined to eat, laugh and mourn together as one for our entire lives.

One night in June 1990, as we were coming home to the Pennington Hostel from Adelaide's city centre on the bus, a man started yelling at us in English.

'This is my land!'

His sounds made us sink into the floor, else we would

have drowned within a minute of swimming in his Aussie accent.

Another night, after returning from her first day in the Pennington Hostel's childcare, Tania remained very quiet. We all sat at the table to eat, drink and talk of the day.

Suddenly Tania spoke. 'I will be mute forever?'

At that moment, I felt a 7.2 magnitude earthquake, so common in Chile. But no water sloshed in our glasses. Our dishes lay motionless on the table. We were already in Adelaide – it was only I that was rattling.

I felt like I was falling into pieces. I wanted to scream, and to continue to fall without a parachute. No passport. Just...*fall*. Back into the prison where I had once lived, instead of the one I was now in. I had put my children in the most modern of prisons – this country where they are today. Looking at us, Tania again asked her question. 'I will stay mute? Because no one speaks Spanish to me here, and I don't know how to speak in English.'

I looked at Lenin, my three-year-old son, as he continued to take his milk and eat bread. Tania cried. We all cried as four castaways from the sound of the Spanish word. Past and present will always be an open wound of not knowing where we belong, where our life dwells versus where our bodies simply exist. We were four new people in this country that someone else calls paradise.

> 'Battle with Foreign Words'
> I am a tree living in a city
> Where people are

I can't speak their languages
I can't write them either…
But I dream every day,
Perhaps I would like to be a poet
I have many leaves that are my eyes,
I see everywhere
My heart is a storehouse for my fruits.

My roots are invisible toes
Stamping on the soil in deep relationship
With worms, ants, snails, and spiders.
Plants, seeds and flowers too
Sharing the great silence of
Our mother earth.

The sun, our father, protects us.
He is always with me,
My brother wind visits me sometimes
And together we dance in the sky,
Or jump over a cloud and swim through
The immense blue.

A glass of water from my sister gives the most
Refreshing liquor
Everyone is equal with the other…
It is not easy to live as a tree
I can't walk,
I have to be here, forever
To survive here is not an easy matter
You have to convince them of who you are

> I am a tree dreaming of being a bird in a nest,
> Inside my poet's heart.

And so began a long struggle with a new language inside a dominant capitalist system when we arrived in Australia. It's a struggle I find parallels the political refugee status that I had and still have, and the experience of not being accepted as a citizen in a country that only accepted its original inhabitants as citizens in 1967.

THE SHAME

I live here in this Aboriginal land, embraced by those who resist this missing acknowledgement and other injustices. Everything for my family – once we chose a pathway of resistance – has been entangled in our skin as if pain were the only sensible thing to celebrate. The empty puppets that we were upon our arrival now know they have human hearts. Connecting with Indigenous Australians was as if another voice from both far or near took our hands and moved us, making us open our eyes, making us laugh and become able to talk about anything.

My family's adaptation to a new life in Australia has remained unfinished ever since we met its Ngarrindjeri people, including my aunties, Veronica and Maggie, and Brother Lionel Fogarty and Sister Ali Cobby Eckermann, Aboriginal resistance poets both. We wished to know their sufferings, dreams and hope. We still do. Where are they? They speak in parks or get lost, eating or getting drunk. Where are *their* dreams and why have they awoken only with a sense of survival and nothing else?

I believe strongly that the Indigenous people of this country have been and will remain the soul of this land exactly as my Mapuche people are to Chile. I believe if we recognise in each other the continuous struggle for justice and freedom, then we can walk and relate in a deeper relationship.

We have learnt to speak the dominant language here in our fight against consumerism because I learnt that our happiness could exist only beyond the consumption of *things*. It was a hard lesson for us to use coin with the face of Her Majesty the Queen in our hands. To us, that feels as if Spain was colonising Chile all over again as we watch on. Even after centuries of slaughter there, we never had to bless and touch their faces in our daily lives.

DAME ROMA MITCHELL GARDENS & ROMERO COMMUNITY

'Cultivate a white rose in April,' said José Martí, an exiled revolutionary and poet who was the primary thinker and father of the Cuban Revolution.

Years of good relationships with friends in the Romero Community came into our lives, and slowly we got to know new fruits of love. It made sense for us to become a part of a new creation, establishing sincere friendships and finding meaning in our existence here where previously there had been none. It was a historical moment – real with spirit and solidarity in resistance. If you have to resist and denounce injustices with words pronounced in vowels and consonants of a dominant power structure you do not understand, that leaves you unhappy and with liabilities you can do nothing about. It was not something that interested us. We turned to gardening: to prepare the land, to plant, to harvest fresh organic vegetables, to look after sheep and chooks, to plant flowers, to prepare compost and, most importantly, to relate to each other with respect and friendship.

I was part of this botanical creation of dignity and hope. It's where homeless men, recovering from life's ills, worked among the smells of the land – our preparation of gardens – fertilising to revive what was ours, those seeds. It helped us grow asparagus among our weeds. Later, we returned to find the colours of a flower, the fruits from our own hands and sweat, that we had planted.

We did not sell our vegetables. Each crop that gave us a dish at the community's table provided fruit to the most marginalised residents of our city via food parcels from the Adelaide Day Centre, our place where Patty (my *companera*) and I worked among others who created this place to care and give dignity to the homeless long before we arrived in Australia. It was in this place that I learnt a lot about Aussie 'mateship' and the acceptance of different cultures into our collective day-to-day work.

Working together in a community garden, being involved with the theatre there and forming real friendships with Australians – people who welcomed us into their lives and into this city – provided joy in our struggles. Tania and Lenin learnt music and became members of a children's theatre group called the Nelson Mandela Theatre Group. Patty and I became part of the Romero Theatre Company, where we performed an annual play directed by Sister Janet Mead. For me, performing here, I was back in Santiago where I studied and acted in works for social justice.

TIEMPO DIFICILES / HARD TIME

During that time I was studying English at the Renaissance Centre in the city's CBD. We worked hard to create a place with Latin American spirit and meaning in our city – a place where history, music, food, poetry and politics were shared with Australian communities. It was because of our own Mapuche, our personal stories of struggle in Southern and Central American countries, that we built a bridge to the local culture. This was our version of Adelaide. But after so many meetings and practicalities, the dream did not survive. One of the reasons why this Latin–American Community Project (Casa Latino America) didn't persist was because, among us Chilean people in Adelaide, there were traitors who did everything to let this project to die. And so it happened.

> Persistence is a seed in our hands
> a resolution in our life
> a relationship in the garden where we work.

Here in Australia, my family continues doing what we left in Chile – making daily 'bread' to share, loaves where the most important ingredients are love and respect for each other. However, to be able to make this bread, I had to know how to understand the instructions, how to read the portion of each ingredient. That is why my studying of English as a second language was essential to the spirit of my poetry.

THE DICTIONARY

I remember how long days were for me to get to any point of understanding the English words which came at me, dark and impenetrable, words I could not even pronounce when I first arrived. I had to take with me everywhere my old dictionary – as though it were a small child fluent in the language of my new land – to engage in *any* dialogue with everyday life. Sometimes my actual children gave me the meaning of the words I needed, just as the new growth from the gardens where I work provides food for those in need. Even now, sometimes I embrace my old dictionary, as if it were my brother Carlos and me reuniting, and we cry together. I remember opening it every day – as if practising a piece of street theatre in Spanish, playing with language and politics on the streets of Santiago. At night, I still feel tired and confused talking to that old dictionary. I wonder if I'll ever be able to translate my current life that flows through my pores and blood; that I *was* and

I remain as this diaspora exile. Will I ever be able to translate my experience of the early 1980s?

'I just want a warm kiss of life without memories of torture and dictators…' *That's* what I mean, as this line from a song by Victor Heredia pleads.

Opening my old dictionary diverts me back onto a painful pathway of memories – putting the book as I once did under my arm as a rebel newspaperman, reading and writing of my experiences in living under a safe house (*Casa de Seguridad*). It is as if I am an old windmill, fighting to twist in the gusts of laughter and opposition, that joy of the road that leads to true humanity and forces us to learn again from our defeated revolution of 1970. But we are still dreaming of turning on the lights anew for that rebellion – in the port of tomorrow's dawn – to bury Allende in our hearts and struggle against the dictator we got and any we might someday endure.

My old dictionary became a mate, helping me to understand the Aussie accent I heard on streets, in hospitals, in Centrelink, and other people's conversations. It provided for me the print words to show what I intended:

> 'The Condor without the Andes'
> Still I can't write perfectly this language
> still I have trouble to pronounce and spell
> more than a hundred words
> still I am learning to swim in your ocean
> but I live on shore and in the land of this country.

Living in Australia without my wings and the wind of the condor – my words and the native language from which they're born – I need to practise the writing and pronunciation of new words I have said hundreds of times before constructing a poem in English. Only then can readers understand how I fly without my mountains here in Australia. But to utter a long, deep love, I come back to the Chile in my mind, saying, 'Thank you, there was a time you gave me water, many seeds of love that still flower in my soul and in my house to avoid my death by uprooting.'

I know I am sinking my *self* into the depths of gum-tree roots. I was there to die and restart my life on a recent morning, having breakfast with all the pain experienced, my pain at its base. Yes, I realise that my wounds are still open as reminders I had to leave my beloved grandparents on their own back in Chile. Even today, my grandmother sleeps in her chair, waiting for my return. Every day, this is her dream.

ABUELO

I open an old suitcase, my grandfather's, and backing up, I see photos of the distance...

I cry. I cry like when my grandfather died. I cry like when I was awarded my humanitarian permanent visa and its condition was not to leave Australia within a two-year span for any reason. The official document from the Military Tribunal Court of Chile 'awarded' me only three months to stay out of Chile – and if I did not return within that term, I would be declared in default and processed in the court with another penalty.

So I didn't come back. I was already one year and half in Australia when my *abuelo* died.

For me, I die now, I die yesterday and I die with my grandfather. I have been sentenced to jail, a graveyard of my own past. Add to this that, before signing any document, I never knew Australia had been invaded by Captain Cook and that he declared this land as a *terra nullius* forever. I would survive in the most modern and sophisticated desert in the world.

Years after my arrival, I read the verses of Fogarty's poem 'Australian Aust:::', which includes these lines near its beginning:

Invasion January 26 2012 still seem terra nullius
Why? For identity look out of just things
Why court lie the years still

One of the saddest experiences we have had was to visit the refugees in the Baxter Detention Centre and Glenside Psychiatric Hospital. Upon each visit I found roots of the damage done to the soul of these people. Their only crime was to believe that Australia is a humanitarian state for everybody. We shared hours of compassion, laughter and hugs – our bodies were soaked in the solitude of their eyes. Their bodies were lying in cables of cruelty where humanity clings in places forgotten. Tania and Lenin, along with other young people, are moved and ashamed to know that this bad treatment of refugees at our door happens in this country.

I have overcome my status as a former political prisoner of Chile's erstwhile dictatorship. I carry with me a poem from Miguel Hernández called 'I Have Three Wounds: Life, Love and Death' as a reminder of my past. But above all, I have overcome the loneliness of exile, its scars of death. I defeated a brutal Pinochet dictatorship – as they wanted to kill the rebel soul and socialist blood in me, as they desired to do within each of the inhabitants of our resistance.

I keep my heart beating with hopes of the red struggle that inspired me to write poetry. I have learnt to overcome the loneliness of Australia, its racist silence and genocide histories. This country that welcomed my family and I – welcomed us to pieces – rendered us dumb and in a pain that has since gradually healed.

I recently saw the film *Pinochet in Suburbia*. It was about an old bastard who made fun of a judicial system, returning to Chile without a scratch on either body or soul with the inhumane political silence of Jack Straw and Tony Blair. We know that there are two justices: one for the rich, which protects the structures of power and domination; a second, more fierce *justicita* for the poor, the indigenous, the refugees and the exiles.

I talk about sharing love and justice for the poor and outcast. It was and remains that love that keeps me rebelling against the apathy of any system that deserves it. This is now my land, too.

CATHERINE REY
To Make a Prairie it Takes a Clover and One Bee

I came to Australia for the wrong reasons.

I settled in Perth in 1997 because one hundred years ago, in January 1913, a country girl from the Charentes in France who had just turned sixteen embarked on a liner in Genoa to join her husband, who had already left France for Perth, Western Australia. Four months earlier, she had given birth to a baby girl who would die within a few weeks. The girl embarking on the liner was my grandmother, my mother's mother.

In one of the photos I have of her, she stands with her two brothers and four sisters. Her parents are seated at the front. She is fifteen in the photo. She is wearing an Alsatian outfit. In 1911, Alsace was the political focus: France wanted to repossess this strip of land annexed by Germany in 1871. Country girls would wear the black Alsatian dress and the large black ribbon attached to the back of their head. Rumours about the war had begun to spread. Did my grandparents leave France because they knew World War I was about to break out? I don't know.

All that I know is that they left: my grandfather first, travelling in horrendous conditions, then his young bride. They were happy in Perth. My grandfather worked at Valencia Wines, in the Swan Valley. My father was born five years later, in Bassendean, in 1918. The couple went back to France in 1928. Why? Nostalgia, sickness, longing to see their family again? Their coming back was a shock. My grandmother used to say that electricity hadn't yet reached the French rural areas, while Bassendean was electrified. I guess their coming back must have been a tragedy. Their going away must have been one, too.

I can hardly imagine this young girl, nearly a child, leaving her country on her own: taking the train to Genoa, falling asleep on the train and being awakened by a gentleman who kindly said, 'Miss, don't forget your boat!' A postcard of Fremantle my grandfather had sent her shows a large cross on the top-left corner. It points out the old Round House, a former jail which stands on top of the hill. My grandfather has written, 'See the cross. I will be there waiting for you.' The girl holds the postcard. She stares at the buildings. She doesn't speak a word of English. She looks forward to seeing her husband again after several months apart, seven weeks at sea – not to mention her baby's death. This is their story. This is my story, too.

I left France for the wrong reasons, to relive the romantic and sad dream of two youngsters who left their country. I wanted to redo step by step their journey, relive their suffering, know exactly what it would have been to leave home before coming back, which must have been heartbreaking and alienating: ignorance and lack of sympathy were typical of those rural areas of the Charentes, and still are. *Australia? Where is that? Do they eat potatoes in Australia?* Many years later, my family still scornfully laughed about Australia. *Australia? Where is that? Do they eat cheese in Australia?* No one was interested in Australia, neither children nor grandchildren. I was the only one to ask questions, for I grew up with my 'Australian' grandparents.

I was the only one to venerate this land across the seas. I knew the 'God Save the Queen' as well as 'La Marseillaise', the French national anthem. I am the only one of four children who sought and was granted Australian citizenship by descent. English was my father's language, my paternal tongue. When my father came back to France, he couldn't speak much French. He was nostalgic for the sandy country he grew up in. Being a 'grasshopper', as his mother used to call him, he didn't like to wear shoes, as with all kids who walk with bare feet.

I left my country, my family, my marriage to live a romantic and mad dream, and to penetrate the mystery I came from. I wanted to understand my grandparents' suffering from the inside, to share it with them and repair an injustice. Writing is my way to comprehend their journey and mine, even though my mystery is overshadowed by theirs. My grandparents had been exiled from their families for unknown reasons. They were first cousins. They married at a very young age.

Their story is the cause of my leaving, romantic and mad, for writers do mad stuff. They never stay quietly within the norms imposed by society, family, school, university, work: writers go astray. This is why they become writers. I wanted to walk through the mirror and break through the secret. And I chucked everything away to do it: my country, my family, my status, my friends and my work.

As a high-school teacher I applied for the five sabbatical years I was allotted. I never went back to my workplace after those five years, which definitively changed the course of my destiny. Then I resigned. Lost, lost in action, I was. I wanted to be reborn, to rewrite my fate and start again from scratch.

My beginnings in life had been a little chaotic. My mother left me with my 'Australian' grandparents when I was three weeks old. Why? Another unanswered question. I wanted to know. This is what writing is for – to pierce mysteries. In a short text relating my departure from France, in July 1997, I wrote: 'I am walking through the boarding gates. I am entering my own death.' I was thirty-nine when I left. My grandmother was sixteen. The same thought would have crossed her mind, not to mention the fear, the indescribable terror of leaving everything and everyone behind. By turning definitively away from my motherland, I violated an interdict and transgressed a taboo. I allowed myself to see the light of day again in order to reinvent my life.

What I found in Perth was unexpected. I quickly felt at home, acquainted with the space, the mores, the people and the streets, even the food. The day I tasted Vegemite, it reminded me of the anchovy paste my grandparents used to buy. The tomato sauce wasn't a surprise, for the 'dead horse' was always enthroned on our French table. I realised that my grandparents had kept eating habits from their Australian past. It was like going back in time. I went straight to Bassendean, but there were no Aboriginal people roaming the bush. In 1912 Indigenous people lived nearby and often asked my grandmother for some fresh water from her garden. Aboriginal people used to live in greater harmony with white people back then: they helped pick grapes in the Swan Valley. Times have changed. The first wooden house my grandparents lived in had been knocked down. A friend of mine, grandnephew of my grandmother's old Parisian–Australian friend, helped me to find their second house. It was still there. I stood at the gate holding the old black-and-white photos. I was moved. I walked inside. I felt at home. I saw a tin bathtub in the garden. I knew it was the original one they had bathed in.

I have gained some understanding of what my grandparents' return could have been like, for I have experienced what it is to go back. The family doesn't show any curiosity about your new homeland. You are expecting questions but they don't ask any. How is my life over there? How do I fill my days? Do I have to drive far to go to work? They don't want to know. For them, my life is tied back to the time when I left their country. This is a movie with many cuts. This is a hand grafted at the level of the shoulder. In between, there is nothing.

This is what going back is all about: to experience the suffering of jumping into a discontinued time when you go back on vacations. Families and friends can handle the huge gap from the moment you leave your country to the time of your return. You can't. They allow no space, no time to talk about this gap in time. All migrant people experience this alienating lack of understanding. It is impossible to feel comfortable in the hole you used to be in before you left. It is hopeless to try to play the same part in the family system. In the end, I burnt nearly all bridges with my past, my relatives, my family and many friends of mine. Communication wasn't possible any longer.

In Australia I found something I wasn't looking for. I found pain. Speaking a foreign language can be a true solitude and a sheer exile. I have often been asked why I wasn't writing in English. That would make my life easier, true, even though the answer seems obvious to me, for I dream, think and write in French before translating my work into English – I can't write in the language of my adopted country. I write in my mother tongue and then translate my work in a two-step process. It started at the university where I taught. Lectures were given in English; I would write them in French before translating them. The day I realised how much the barrier of language was cruelly isolating me, I started thinking that I could write novels in English by this method as well.

English is the language with which I communicate. It remains a useful and a practical tool I use, as would a pair of pliers. When two of my novels were translated, I was glad to share my world and my words and to remove the barrier of the language. But English cannot be my creative language; there is an intimate space in the creator's mind, which is the very space where thoughts come to life: it is formless, made of dreams and reveries, of memories surging from the past. From the inner discourse when one is talking to oneself or when one is dreaming, thoughts emerge slowly and bear each other; ideas rise from a word one has come across while reading *in the mother tongue*, and that very word brings suddenly back a whole piece of the buried past, childhood memories, an acute vision of an old house; a forgotten sound, forgotten smell, the forgotten blue of a wisteria, suddenly vivid and alive. Recently reading *Feu de Feuilles* by Alain Galan, I experienced an unexpected trance when I came across the word *étude de notaire:* notary's office... My mother had her own real estate agency. When she would take me to town, which wasn't very often as she was very busy working, we used to go to the notary's office to pick up or drop off some paperwork. Stumbling across the word *étude*, I immediately remembered the smell of ink in this dusty world of cabinets of drawers, pencil cases and boxes, well before the time of computers. Most of all it reminded me of my mother, her hand awkwardly holding mine; our rare outings, our silences. This is pure inspiration to me. The words I use are closely linked to my body's memory, deeply rooted in my unconscious. And the unconscious is spoken, lived and written in the mother tongue.

I didn't come to Australia until I was thirty-nine; thus I will always remain exterior to my own speech. My feeling of estrangement derives from the fact that my body doesn't inhabit English. I rarely forget about this icy space between my words and my soul. Suddenly thrown in the midst of an unfamiliar topic, I drown, submerged by information I don't understand. Making an inquiry on the telephone can quickly turn into a nightmare, especially if I have to spell my name. On the other end of the telephone line is a voice humming a stream of words, and there is nothing coating the sound, just noise devoid of meaning. This frustrating situation always brings me back to the pain of being excluded. I am and will remain a foreigner. In a conversation, I nod. I pretend. But sooner or later something gives me away. A joke I don't get. My humour dies. Joking isn't for me. It requires being witty, fast; here is a wealth of words to play with, but in my adopted country, I don't play with words. I use them as a practical tool. I use them to be understood.

Double alienation and double pain when my turn to speak comes: beyond the words, I am referring to some historical fact – the May 1968 revolution, for instance, when French society was turned upside down. A mention of Daniel Cohn-Bendit, nicknamed 'Danny the Red', would be immediately understood by my peers, my people, my friends and my generation. At work I might like to quote the name of a respected art critic, George Didi-Huberman, or a famous contemporary author I admire, Pascal Quignard, but they are only respected or famous 'over there', in my home country. Iraqis and Iranians who work with me experience the same lack of understanding: they speak, but their speech drifts away. Nobody acknowledges what has been said. No one reacts. They have nevertheless referred to an important name, a major historical event, a war, a massacre everyone knew – but *only* important 'over there'. Iraqis know better than I do what war, massacre and forced exile mean. If they mention the name of a famous Sufi mystic respected by every single person in their motherland, they experience the same silence. No one in Australia has ever heard of it. Me neither. I have caught the involuntary look of despair they immediately wipe off their face. Listeners behave as though they have blown wisps of smoke. There is a polite silence and just the smoke of our words blowing from our mouth. Silence. No echo. No resonance. Transparent swirls: this is our speech. Us, immigrants, people who migrated to Australia at a mature age, people with a past – we silence our past as we have learnt this cruel rule: immigrants have no past.

I have rediscovered my voice. In the five novels I have written in Australia, I have granted myself many licences with my idiom. France's literary world is judgemental. There my baroque style – a mix of words prosaic and lyrical, peasant sayings, neologisms; nothing like classical – can be seen as over the top. I would call this style my third language, my creolised language. Talking and writing require different skills, though. As I sit in front of my page, there is no hazard. I move in slow motion. I am safe within the intimate citadel of my familiar French words. My mother tongue is my homeland. The rarity of my mother tongue, since I have hardly any opportunity to practice it, has made French very precious. I value it. At the same time I enjoy the challenging but rewarding solitude of being far away from my peers. Being cut off from influences means no trend. No judgemental look over my shoulder. No superego. No questions like 'What will they think of me?' Being far away from one's native country allows you to be stripped of the old self. The 'English graft', to borrow Andreï Makine's word, has enriched my French. Over my last five novels, my voice has changed. How could I have forgotten the stunning experience of writing *The Spruiker's Tale*? It all started in 2001 with *Lucie Comme les Chiens,* when I decided to talk from the point of view of a mentally disabled young woman. Why? I viewed myself that way in my new homeland.

I grew up in France with my 'Australian' grandparents, as I have said. One morning while we were having breakfast, my grandmother and I noticed my grandfather's confusion. My grandmother questioned him. He finally confessed that he had had a dreadful nightmare. After I pressed him to reveal his dream, he uttered that in it I had been cut in half; then, the poor man, he buried his face in his hands, invoking the Good Lord...

'Was I cut in the middle or from top to bottom?' I asked, ignoring the gruesome description. As a young person who had just read Freud's *The Interpretation of Dreams*, nightmares didn't frighten me.

'From top to bottom!' he muttered.

What a significant dream you had, my dear poppy, foreseeing the story of my life: half here, half there – living between Mother France and Father Australia and writing in between their tongues.

SHALINI AKHIL
Home and (Take)Away

The overwhelming sense of wonder I felt when I unwrapped my first Cornetto in Melbourne sticks with me to this day. How I marvelled at its preciseness – the cool white of the expertly piped ice-cream, tiny chocolate rivulets snap-frozen in its ridges and valleys. And the crunch! It seemed just one bite of the waffle cone could trigger an avalanche – similar, perhaps, to the controlled avalanches they set off in the Cornetto factory to send golden nut fragments cascading down to lodge themselves into the waiting ice-cream mountains before they are wrapped and shipped to people like me? I remember wondering if everyone who unwrapped a Cornetto took the time to admire its perfection before devouring it; I certainly hoped they did.

It's not like I'd never had a pre-packaged, cone-shaped, single-serve ice-cream before the age of eighteen. Nothing makes you more appreciative of the small stuff than a spell spent away from them.

I am the youngest of three children. I was born in Fiji, and spent the first six months of my life there. I moved with my family to Australia, where my father was to study Law. We lived first in Townsville, then in Sydney until I was eight. Shortly after attending Dad's graduation ceremony, we packed up our things and went back to my birthplace: Lautoka, situated on the west coast of Fiji's main island, Viti Levu. Ten years later, in 1991, I moved to Melbourne to stay with my brother in Caulfield. This is where the Cornetto-love episode took place.

I've always been obsessed with ice-cream, and have worked out that my first memory is of waiting in high anticipation for someone – my dad and brothers, most likely – to return from the milk bar with Paddle Pops. I must have been tiny, unable to walk yet, but I clearly remember flailing around on the floor in a long, narrow hallway, straining to look back over my shoulders at the upside-down screen door, waiting eagerly for familiar shadows to bob into view and cut through the brightness. It's since been confirmed that the hallway in my memory belonged to the weatherboard we rented in Townsville. I believe the flavour I was waiting for was banana (still my favourite).

The Cornetto equivalent in Fiji is the Drumstick. Unwrapped, it *looked* like a Cornetto, and its elements were the same – but there the similarities ceased. In my Fijian childhood ice-cream experiences, you'd have been hard-pressed to find a Drumstick with the clean, precise lines of a Cornetto.

Let me introduce you to the concept of 'Fiji time'. The ever-present heat and humidity saps just enough energy to slow the pace of life down to a comfortable amble, so while things get done, they get done in their own sweet time. Fiji time affects every aspect of life over there – even the Drumstick. When you unwrapped one there, you'd most likely be greeted by a slightly misshapen crown of ice-cream. The chocolate rivers smudging these valleys showed evidence of having broken the banks; the chocolate and the ice-cream would have melded together and re-frozen multiple times in transit from the factory to the shop. But of course you'd press on, braving the compromised slopes to discover ice-cream where the ice and the cream were often separately identifiable in each bite. Finally, the clincher: a *chewy* waffle cone.

Like the Drumsticks in my home town, memories are hard things to anticipate when they're only just being formed. A soggy-shelled ice-cream is certainly not something I thought I'd crave later on in life. But the things I miss about Fiji have less to do with preciseness, efficiency or even sanitation, and more to do with authenticity.

One of my favourite after-school snacks was sweet tea, accompanied by puffy chilli-and-garlic pappadums – we'd buy them by the bagful off this lady who lived in town. They were sun-dried, and you knew this because you'd have to pick your way carefully through them as you made your way across her front lawn to her door. When we went to Churchill Park for school sports days, my friends and I used to buy hand-rolled, chilli-sugar-salt tamarind balls from this old lady who would set up 'shop' on an old mat spread at the edge of the oval.

While the line of comparison between a Drumstick and a Cornetto was pretty easily drawn, Melbourne has surprised me with some accidental discoveries in the past, eliciting a jolt of memory so powerful that I've been instantly transported across the Pacific on a mere whiff.

The first time I walked past a vendor selling roast chestnuts on a busy street corner in the middle of Melbourne, the aroma took me straight back to the kitchen of the house I'd left when I moved here, the house my parents were still living in. Rushing past people on my way to somewhere I was expected on a cold, mid-week winter's day, I was suddenly enveloped by a smoky, sweet smell so out of context that I had to stop and seek its source. It was a smell I'd turned my nose up at many times before. Back then I didn't know that *naibi* were chestnuts native to Fiji: all I knew was that if a bag of them turned up at our house, there would be much excitement. Everyone else in my family was crazy about them – me, not so much. Even so, the smell of *naibi* cooking was not something I was expecting to encounter in the middle of the day on a Melbourne street corner. I made my way through the rush of people to the vendor and, even though I knew I didn't really like them, I bought a bag of roast chestnuts. And ate them. Slowly.

While I still work in the city, I've now settled in the west. Footscray has been very good to me in the five years my husband and I have lived here. Everything I need to throw together a close-to-authentic home-style meal –

masala mix, ground turmeric, dhal and ghee, goat meat, duck meat, you name it – I can source it from within a one-kilometre radius of my house. This contrasts sharply with my memories of a time when vegetables impossible to find in Melbourne were smuggled to Australia in luggage – chopped up raw, tumbled in turmeric and bagged, they'd be passed off at Customs as cooked.

While my father was studying in Queensland in 1966 – a Bachelor of Commerce he would abandon after the first year – my mother was expecting my oldest brother. Her first pregnancy, so far away from home, came with some very specific and far-away cravings: she wanted *chauraiya bhaji* – a kind of spinach green common in Fiji, usually fried simply with onion, garlic and chilli and eaten with roti or rice. But Queensland in 1966 was not at all like Footscray in 2013. Dad had no idea how or where to get his hands on some for her. That is, until one day when he noticed familiar-looking 'weeds' growing around the fence line of the units they lived in. On closer inspection, he was confounded – *chauraiya bhaji* in his own backyard! He harvested what he could and made a beeline for the landlady, who lived in a unit in the complex. He showed her the leaf, assured her that he was not trying to kill his wife by feeding her weeds, and asked if she could possibly instruct the gardener to not mow them.

It was in Footscray that I discovered you could order coconut water by the glass at almost any Asian restaurant. It's served chilled, a generous serving of scooped slivers of silky coconut flesh nestled at the base of the glass. I grew up on the stuff, consumed directly from young green nuts picked off the palm. Now I can re-create that memory any time I want by popping a straw into a chilled can, closing my eyes, and sipping.

I'll never forget that night when, after post-work drinks, we stumbled, starving, out of Footscray station and straight into the Indian takeaway across the road. There, staring up at me from a bain-marie in all its oil-slicked glory was the most authentic South Indian goat curry I had tasted in years. The smell of it took me back to my dad's office on a Saturday when we'd get the goat curry lunch-plate from City Takeaway in Lautoka. It was seriously so good I tweeted.

We stumbled upon another discovery mid-hangover. When my husband returned from our local Vietnamese bakery one Sunday with my regular request of *banh mi* (with extra chilli) and a bottle of the Black Doctor (Coke – *never* Diet), he also handed me a lumpy paper bag. I was in no mood for surprises – which made the resulting discovery even sweeter. The paper bag yielded what looked like a naked, lumpy cupcake that certainly wasn't trying too hard to sell itself. I almost didn't eat it, but my husband insisted. That first bite stays with me still – chewy at the edges, spongy and dense within – the taste was so familiar that it kind of freaked me out. I've since foisted them on family and watched eagerly for the wide-eyed flicker of recognition on that first bite. *Vakalolo*, a Fijian sweet made of grated taro, coconut milk and sugar, had found me in Footscray (via Vietnam), hand delivered by an Irish–South African–Australian husband who had no idea he was about to spark a new take on an old obsession – *Vakalolo* 2.0.

I don't think I'd eaten as much *jalebi* in the ten years I spent in Fiji – where it is so common – as I have so far in Melbourne. *Jalebi* is an Indian sweet that looks like a cartoon scribble made with bright orange texta. To make it, a thin batter is quickly piped into boiling ghee in a circular motion, deep fried till crispy, then dunked immediately in simmering sugar syrup. The result is what I imagine Enid Blyton's pop biscuits would taste like: a crunch followed by flowing sugar syrup. My family is well-versed in the delights of fresh *jalebi*. I once even took a box full of them to work and dispensed them from desk to desk. Nothing gives me more joy than watching the uninitiated bite into something delicious for the first time.

Moving to another country will make you more resourceful. My family have always been avid picklers; they love to preserve things – to catch them at the perfect stage of sweetness or sourness and bottle them up. Due to its over-abundance in Fiji, it was all about mango. Fresh green mangoes are perfect for pickling; smothered in a mix of salt, chilli, crushed garlic, ground fenugreek and mustard oil, mango *achar* makes for a sharp and crunchy accompaniment for rice and dhal – or eaten one after the other unaccompanied, until your mother orders you to stop. My parents found apples to be a perfect stand-in, and they do the job well – but nothing beats a fresh mango.

Looking back, I never would have known I'd get all misty-eyed at the memory of the mango tree in our front yard at the height of the season. That tree was like a stealth bomber, laden with mangos so ripe and juicy that burst on contact like warm, sticky water balloons when they dropped. Pulp puddles, fruit flies, air tinged with sweet decay – what's not to miss? Nowadays if I want a hit, Footscray Markets in the summertime can suffice, for both the fruit and the funk.

There is, however, one craving I'm yet to satisfy – I haven't had it in so long that I occasionally dream about it: coconut flower. There's a time in a coconut's life-cycle where it grows past the point of being a useful, edible fruit and crosses over into its duty – becoming a seed for a new coconut palm. When shaken, the coconut sounds hollow and waterless, and sometimes a white mass appears in one of the 'eyes' at its base. Upon cracking the nut open, you find the inside filled with what looks like a spongy balloon. It has a texture like Styrofoam and is the sweetest thing I've ever tasted.

For the moment, I'm happy to live with the memory – if experience has taught me anything, it's that a coconut flower will find its way to me when I'm least expecting it. It probably won't look like a coconut flower, or be encased in a coconut shell like I'd expect it to be – but when I taste it, I'll know.

VAL COLIC-PEISKER
Deliberations of a Reasonably Domesticated Immigrant

In a hundred years' time, long flights in economy class will be considered a cruel practice of the late twentieth and early twenty-first centuries. Australians are no doubt the main sufferers: we are a wealthy country at the end of the world (depending, of course, where one places its centre), close only to Indonesia and a few Pacific islands. Therefore, Australian middle classes compulsively travel to northern metropolises for business and fun, and as therapy for the 'cultural cringe', bravely submitting themselves to the sitting-up torture of economy class. I defy the tyranny of distance in this inelegant way more often than most, with the additional excuse of 'going home'.

On my last trip to Europe I arrived at Heathrow airport in better shape than usual after being sardined in a huge, filled-to-the-last-seat, double-decker Airbus for thirteen hours. I attempted running up and down the stylishly curved stairs as the best available exercise, but a cheerless sleep-deprived hostess – it was the dead of night – ordered me back to my seat. I often admire the stoicism of the unfortunate economy-class passengers, meekly sticking to their seats, remaining civil (mostly) to each other and the crew. No one kicks or screams, no one goes berserk: what an achievement of civilisation! And I do envy those who can sleep tight, peacefully snoring in the most impossible, uncomfortable positions.

The lack of sleep makes Heathrow's grungy charm – in contrast to Singapore's spotless airport – seem more depressing than of historical interest. The old world versus the new. A passport-control officer was chewing gum and did not say hello. The bus trip from Heathrow to Cambridge took three hours, as if I needed more travelling. That was a poor, uninformed decision – I should have taken a train. My first day in Cambridge was free from official program, so I rented a bicycle and rode around the famous little city. I noticed the grass was lush and green, and there's lots of it everywhere. The cars were smaller than in Ozland, as size is inversely proportional to the petrol price. Over lunch in a packed restaurant, I noticed many Cambridge ladies are what continental Europeans would label as 'badly dressed'. They seemed unconcerned about looking 'stylish' and attractive – a sign of depressive illness, or perhaps of gender equality (Germaine Greer, are you reading this?) and the emancipation from vanity? Some of this tradition has been transplanted to Australia, but there are pockets of stylish resistance – Melbourne likes to think of itself as one.

Don't get me wrong: I am not some conceited Eurocentric. After my initial culture shock, I came to greatly appreciate the relaxed Australian dress codes. It was explained to me when I first arrived that if an Australian man appears to dress up or matches colours too well, he *must* be gay. Straight men dress as if they slipped into whatever clothes they could find in the dark. Whereas in my native Croatia, men can wear shorts in hot summer *only* if a) they are under twenty-five or b) they have fantastic legs. Middle-aged women are not allowed to go downtown in cargo pants – it's not against the law, but well-meaning friends would tell them off. This happened to me during my last visit. My smartly dressed friend gave me a worried look and asked: 'Are you going to town *like this*?' I didn't want her to be embarrassed in my company so I pulled a pair of linen trousers out of my suitcase. More ironing to do…

In Croatian cities, people's self-esteem and social status depend partly on their grooming, and the rules are rather strict about what is an appropriate outfit for any particular occasion. How many hours of my life I spent ironing silk blouses and linen jackets! And what an inordinate portion of my then much-smaller income was spent on clothes. My realisation that the Australian fashion rules were much more laissez-faire came with a true sense of liberation. I could now go to a supermarket in my tracksuit. Smart feminine shoes that once gave me bunions are now only worn on special occasions. I am also cured of my 'nothing to wear' neurosis. I only ever feel underdressed in Zagreb or my native Rijeka when

I meet my perfectly dressed and coiffed girlfriends. But I know the price of that, and I do not envy them.

◆

Overall, England was nice to me on this occasion. The weather gods made an exceptional effort with several picture-perfect sunny days in early spring. My presentation on new developments in Australian multiculturalism at Reading University was well received, with unexpected high praise by an official from the Australian High Commission in London. On our way to a pre-arranged workshop lunch he confessed he could not wait to go back home to Canberra. A proud Australian who prefers Canberra to London — well, someone has to like Canberra too! I can be counted among the people for whom London is just a bit too much of a good thing. Samuel Johnson famously proclaimed that 'if one has tired of London, one is tired of life'. Well…

On my first visit to London, last century, I was sightseeing tirelessly: my most comfortable pair of shoes (at that time, golden sandals) ended in a bin after four days of walking in the rain. I had to see all the places from my high-school English textbook. But my sightseeing stamina is much less these days: I am not a wide-eyed youth anymore. I forced myself into a tiny bit of sightseeing on this most recent trip, out of courtesy toward the city's grand reputation. I made it to

Trafalgar Square, pondered life for a while at the stairs of the National Gallery, then decided not to enter. I confirmed what I already knew: ninety-nine per cent of all monuments in the imperial city are in honour of military men, of their conquests and sacrifices for the homeland. Not my cup of English Breakfast tea. I met two colleagues in London, one Russian and one Serbian, for lunch and dinner respectively. Nice and interesting women, each working at a different London university, one partnered with an Englishman and the other with a Frenchman. Ah, multiculturalism, globalisation, isn't it all fabulous, I thought after a glass of wine.

Indeed, we're in the age of migration – especially down here in Ozland. My hyper-mobility suggests I acculturated well enough. Last year in Florence I had the pleasure of hearing a small Chinese child rabbiting on in *alta velocità* Italian. A few weeks before this, I had the pleasure of seeing a little Tamil child pedalling on a tricycle across the road and bringing a large tourist bus to a halt – in the Lofoten Islands, the land of the Vikings, beyond the Arctic circle in Norway. So perhaps my being in Australia is not all that strange. Although I sometimes find myself surprised.

Ha! I live in Melbourne, Australia!
How did that happen?

They gave me the Australian passport, a job, and they even ask me to write about it.
Nice people!

I've been in Australia for seventeen years and by now I am reasonably domesticated. However, my good Anglo-Australian mates still sometimes wince when I say *exactly* what I think. That's perhaps the most serious flaw in my acculturation record: I never mastered polite restraint and the (in)famous Anglo understatement. I think I am temperamentally unsuited to it. That's why I always proofread my emails before clicking on 'Send' – not so much for typos as for bluntness. It is harder to keep oneself in check face-to-face. I am sure I have lifted many eyebrows over the years. Diversity is easier to praise than practice.

Although much less often than when I first arrived here, people still ask me where I am from and why I came to Australia. Do I like it here? The most recent time this happened to me was only a month ago at Richmond train station, by a complete stranger apparently behaving in a rather un-Australian fashion: Anglos do not usually show interest in strangers at railway stations.

I said I was coming from Armadale. 'Yes,' he insisted, 'but where do you *originally* come from?'

I have been asked these types of questions so many times I am thoroughly bored by them. I know people mean no harm – it is something to talk about and sometimes there is genuine interest – but after answering them repeatedly, I am no longer able to make myself utter the same sentences in reply. So I have started making things up. When you chat to someone at a large suburban party there is a decent chance you'll never see them again, so they'll never find out you are not really from Novosibirsk, Russia – even more so if you have been accosted for impromptu questioning at a suburban train station.

My accent is Slavic. It can pass for Russian, especially with Aussies, whose foreign language expertise is usually rudimentary. During my first year in Australia, an amateur theatre asked me to record a play they were rehearsing with a Russian accent (as it was a Russian story). That's where I got the Siberia idea. 'But I'm not Russian!' I protested. 'Oh, but you have a beautiful Russian accent.' Oh, well then. Why split hairs? I read it using my hardest Slavic *Rrr*. They ate it up.

I am not a formal type of person and I happily picked up Australian slang – even some of the Australian twang, according to my Canadian and English colleagues. I know what people who are 'built like a brick shithouse' look like and what a 'dunny' is. I can say 'whaddayareckon' pretty convincingly, but the general strictures of Strine phonetics will forever be beyond me. And as to understanding Strine speakers, it took considerable time getting used to. It was only after six months that I began understanding anything at all.

I could speak English before moving to Australia, but the hard-core version of Strine came as a surprise. My listening-comprehension problem was exacerbated by the fact that speakers of Strine think they're speaking English and it is a matter of politeness to leave them in that conviction. But regardless of my linguistic development I'll never be able to hide my immigrant tracks.

The first twelve years of my Australian life I spent in Perth – perhaps the sunniest city on earth. I soon realised, in that grumpy ungrateful Southern European way, that endless sunshine is not all that great. The Australian summer sun is strong enough to be outright dangerous. The British love Perth for its weather, and contribute significantly to the national skin cancer statistics by overcompensating for the climate they suffered in the old country – but I digress.

Our first house was a duplex in a quiet suburb close to the beach. Perth is in fact an oversized collection of quiet suburbs close to the beach. We arrived in early January and before long I learnt that summer in Perth comes adorned with large, red, flying cockroaches. So instead of frightening my five-year-old son with piercing screams – my instinctive reaction to large cockroaches – I rang our landlord (who spoke medium-hard Strine) and complained. He said he'd send someone from the Water Authority (he worked there) to call in and spray the water mains. And indeed, a day later, the doorbell rang. A tall bloke in small shorts (good legs) and boots was at the door.

This was my first encounter with authentic unadulterated Strine. It went like this:

He: G'day. Oi sars pray yer wortamayns fe cockies.
Me: Silence...
He: Wears ya wortamayns?
Me: Are you asking me where the water main is?
He: Hey lady, arya kiddinme?
I understood the last sentence.

I politely explained to him that I had been in Australia for only two weeks and could not understand the Australian accent. He gave me a strange look and went to the edge of the front garden for the killing spree.

At that early stage my English was not only 'foreign' but also way too formal – learnt in school and never practised with native speakers in everyday life. I referred to the 'front door' as the 'entrance' and to 'a couple of kids' as 'two children'. On a mission to buy some second-hand furniture in my new neighbourhood, I encountered several children playing in the front garden:

'Excuse me, children, where is the entrance?'

'Paaardon?'

'Where's the entrance, please?'

'What? What does she want?'

'Aah,' one of them says, 'she's asking about the front door!'

Yes, the bloody front door!

Well, no, of course I did *not* say that final line. I like children. I am just showing off the progress I've made with the language. These days when I inquire about prices in shops it is by 'emma chisit?' No one's ever replied, 'Beg'y'pardon?'

Why I came to Australia and whether I like it here, I cannot say anymore. It's been too long and both questions require far longer answers than what I can offer here. The answer to the second question would depend on the day and my mood. And please do not ask me whether I feel more Croatian or more Australian. I do not feel particularly defined by my 'ethnicity' or 'culture'. Some days, when I listen to my favourite CDs, I feel Italian. Sometimes French. Last time I read Dostoyevsky I pined for St Petersburg.

But I can say that I now find my native Croatia somewhat 'exotic', filled with people with unexpected attitudes doing things the odd way; the way I probably did them once upon a time. I find Croatian food generally too rich, as I am now converted to Asian cuisines. My old friends have changed, and it would make full sense that I've changed even more. Fewer of them smoke these days, but some still do. In any case, we are somewhat weird to each other after almost two decades.

Those who persisted in remaining my friends find the differences amusing, but some old friendships have not withstood the widening cultural gap. My old mates find me 'businesslike' and 'hyperactive'. I admit I simply cannot spend hours on end sitting in coffee shops, even when I'm 'on holidays'. I hasten to add that Croatian coffee shops are first-class – but the languid, idle-away-hours lifestyle is simply not me anymore, if it ever was.

HSU-MING TEO
Here and There and Over the Sea to Sky

HERE, 1978

I did not know then there was a place called Skye. I knew only that there was sky – a loud, shouting blue grazed with wisps of white and breathing heat. I did not know that there was a man called Bonnie Prince Charlie, and even if I had I would not have known why he was bonnie or on the way to Skye. I did not know much. I was not yet eight years old and an immigrant to Australia.

But as I perched on the stiff leather saddle of the bicycle, fists tightly gripping the handlebars, I knew the wind slapping at my face and tearing at my hair. I knew the diamond shapes of the cyclone fence along Cumberland Avenue, Castle Hill. It cut off the orange orchard from the tidy gardens with their landscaped rockeries and the double-storeyed brick-veneer houses marching up the street. We lived in the house at the top of the hill. Sometimes there were ponies in the orchard, because the Hills district was still rural back then. Sometimes the farmer was there, twisting off oranges and dropping them into baskets. In the early mornings he whistled a tune and waved us off to school. A red mesh bag of green-tinged oranges appeared on our veranda during our first Christmas in Australia.

There was no Christmas tree yet, but there was a dull gold bicycle in the garage. It was a Malvern Star – not quite what I'd hoped for. I wanted a girly bike, lilac-coloured, with tassels streaming from the handlebars and a white wicker basket sprouting pink and yellow daisies. Instead, my father bought me a sturdy bike with an adjustable seat that would last long after I'd outgrown the desire for plastic tassels and fake flowers. It looked like a boy's bike, but it would do. At that time, I was reading the popular English children's author Enid Blyton. I devoured her Adventure Series, and I learnt about the Faraway Tree in the Enchanted Wood. I wanted to cycle into a forest; I wanted adventures. There was a scrubby reserve on Tuckwell Road at the end of Cumberland Avenue. That would do, too.

My feet couldn't quite touch the cement floor of our double garage, and at first the bike tipped from side to side. When my mother had hung out the laundry, she came into the garage and gripped the back of the bicycle seat so that my feet could rest on the pedals. We went round and round the garage until I could balance. I was ready to ride my bike on the street, ready for adventures in this new country that I knew nothing about. This was not the imaginary England of Enid Blyton, but it too would do.

There was exhilaration and sheer joy of motion and of speed. Melding with the bike I became a machine splicing the air, my legs pumping like pistons. I was sailing downhill and there was nothing to do but glide, soar, and sing the song I was learning at school:

> Speed, bonnie boat, like a bird on the wing,
> Onward! the sailors cry;
> Carry the lad who's born to be King
> Over the sea to Skye.

At some point I realised I did not know how to control the bike. I did not know how to steer, how to turn a corner; frozen with fear, I forgot how to stomp back on the pedals to brake. I was gliding, soaring, speeding, rush-rush-rushing towards a caravan parked at the end of the road.

I didn't see the street, the houses or the orchard anymore. All I could see was that white caravan looming closer – then with a thumping crash and the clattering of metal, I was tossed up over the handlebars.

I looked up into an infinity of blue. Then, pain everywhere. I couldn't move my left arm. I lay on my broken bicycle waiting for someone to come. I thought of where I'd come from before I flew over the sea to sky.

THERE, 1977

Classes in my primary school in Petaling Jaya, Malaysia, began at 7.30 in the morning, so I had to wake up in the dark, fumble on my white shirt and yank the starched navy pinafore over my head. 'Be very quiet,' the maid said, 'your parents are still asleep.' Sometimes there was congee with fried anchovies and peanuts for breakfast, sometimes kaya toast, and sometimes there was a soft-boiled egg congealing in a pink bowl, swimming in soy sauce with white pepper sprinkled over the glistening yolk. I had to eat quickly so that I wouldn't miss the bus that picked up all the kids along our street.

Each day the maid helped me lace up my white tennis shoes. She unlocked the high metal gate and dragged me out to wait in front of its vertical bars. The streetlights blinked and shut their eyes and then…grey morning. No aubade to welcome the dawn, no gradual transition from night into day. It was still cool, though, the air almost fresh. A few hours later, when we were parading around the schoolyard in endless, pointless drills, the air would be damp and pulpy like slow-rotting fruit, layered with smell upon lush smell: putrefying rubbish spilling out of metal bins; the choking fumes of trucks rumbling along the highway; the sharp, sweet scent of petrol slicked on bitumen; the pungent odours of *rempah* sizzling in oil and curries from the canteen; the stench of sweating bodies smothered in hot uniforms; and the faintest snap of ozone from the coming afternoon thunderstorm.

We marched and marched, then stood in orderly rows to sing the Malaysian national anthem. *Negara ku, tanah tumpahnya darah ku…* 'My country, my native land…' Except it wasn't, because I wasn't Malay. I didn't speak or understand Malay. I was an ethnic Chinese girl who read Enid Blyton and my mother always insisted she belonged to Singapore.

I hated my first year of primary school because my teacher was a screamer and a scolder with a wooden ruler that she smacked on her metal-framed desk when she was angry. She was angry about many things, especially questions. 'What is your name?' she shouted. I was too scared and too shy to answer. I didn't do well with people who yelled.

> *Don't you even know your name, you stupid girl?*
> *What is seventeen plus eight?*
> *How many points does the star have in the Jalur Gemilang?*
> *Don't you know that's the Malaysian flag?*
> *How many stripes for each state?*
> *What is the time now?*
> *Can't you even tell the time?*
> *Say good morning in Bahasa and don't mumble. Speak up!* Selamat pagi, Bu!

Once I stole a Parker pen from my father's office and an apple from the fridge to appease the teacher. I read far too many English storybooks as a child.

But it wasn't all about school, of course. There were lavish birthday parties, for which my parents hired steel swings, slides, merry-go-rounds and lots of little chairs and tables for my school friends and the neighbourhood kids. There were birthday cakes shaped like trains, ducks and even a grand piano. There were book-buying trips to the local department store and visits to fabric shops, where bolts of coloured cloth lined the walls and leaned out of cardboard boxes. Sometimes there were excursions to Petaling Street in Kuala Lumpur, where my mother took us to see where she worked, in the dental surgery, before taking us for lunch: wonton or beef-ball noodles. At night my father strapped us into the back of his vermilion Mercedes and cruised the streets of Petaling Jaya looking for wok-charred black KL Hokkien mee and durians.

There was my brother – just a toddler then – making us sing 'Happy Birthday' to all his toys at night before he went to bed. We played with his rocket and his Tonka truck and building blocks. In the garden, surrounded by tea-tree hedges, we bounced a pink ball between us and got scolded by the maids for running our hands in the drain water. Once, a man came to remove a brown snake from the water cistern. He gripped it under its head and showed it to us, looped around his wrist and forearm. And there was also the peanut seller, tooting away on the rubber horn of his bicycle. He scooped up salt-crusted peanuts into cones made out of sheets of the Yellow Pages and we chorused *terima kasih*! as he handed them to us.

But then the house was sold and we got on a plane and flew over the sea to sky.

HERE, 1978

It was my first summer, the first time I saw yellowing grass and scraggly trees with brown-tipped leaves. At night cicadas chirred and shrilled in pulsing discord. Running around the backyard during the day, my brother and I sometimes heard the crunch of their brittle husks breaking under our thongs. I liked to pick up the empty shells and lift them to the sun, bug-eyed aliens haloed with light and brightness pouring through the bronze-veined fairy wings. It was baking hot, with no relief from the westerly wind that huffed like a dragon's breath and scorched my skin.

My mother turned on the sprinkler and my brother hollered as he bounded through the snorts of swirling water, sliding over the wet green garbage bags she had pegged to the lawn. I could only watch. I had a heavy plaster cast around my left forearm where the bone had snapped. I hugged it close to my chest in a white cotton sling. Most of the time the arm did not feel like it belonged to me. I hated its weight and the prickly sweat that pooled under the bandage, trapped in that hot, damp tomb.

Mrs Holden had a pool and an idea. She was our neighbour three houses up the adjoining road and I had become friends with her daughter, Nora. When we first moved in, she made a curry and brought it round to welcome us to the neighbourhood. We were so grateful, but we were also surprised to find grapes bobbing around in the watery gravy. To us, 'curry' meant gluggy brown *rendangs* that looked like lumps of turd and tasted like home. I loved the Holdens' house because it had a mock-Tudor facade and rose bushes by the door. The Holdens' house looked like what I thought a house in the West would, from the illustrations in my storybooks. There was a fibreglass swimming pool cut into the lawn, though, and that was not in any book I'd read.

One particularly hot afternoon, after a lunch of fairy bread and store-bought lamingtons – very exotic to me then – Mrs Holden wrapped my cast in two Fielder's white-bread plastic bags and secured the tops with string. I could go for a paddle in the pool, she said, but I had to take care to keep my arm out of the water. I didn't, of course; the string came loose and water seeped into the bread bags. By the time I climbed out of the pool, my cast was soaked and my parents would be home in three hours. I rushed home to my bedroom, turned on the small fan heater and sat in front of it, drying my cast with the glare of the afternoon sun slanting in through the venetian blinds. I kept away from pools and sprinklers alike for the rest of the summer.

Then it was back to school and I wasn't in Nora's class. I was scared. But there was no shouting teacher here in the stuffy demountable classroom with the aluminium walls and the green felt carpet covering the steel rivets bolting the sections of the building together. Instead, there was sandy-haired, bearded Mr Lyne, who taught us to play The Carpenters' 'Sing, Sing a Song' on our bone-coloured plastic recorders so that he could sing along with his guitar perched on his knee. He liked to play his guitar on Friday afternoons when there was no point in learning anything, with the weekend just a school-bell ring away. His whole body would dip and sway as he strummed, tapped the frets, rapped his knuckles on the pick guard of his guitar and sang the Peter, Paul and Mary version of 'Oh, Rock My Soul (in the bosom of Abraham)'. He was my favourite teacher, because he showed me that I didn't have to be afraid.

In later years, when I was older and more attuned to these things, there was a period when I occasionally heard young men on the train calling out to me and other Asians: 'Ching-Chong-Chinaman', 'dirty Chink', 'slanty eyes' and 'fuckinasiangohome.' It all seems rather dated these days, and it never really bothered me back then because home was now Here, not There. Here there was the orange farmer, Mrs Holden and Nora, Mr Lyne and so many more. I don't know where they are now, but I am so lucky to have known them all when I first flew over the sea to sky and landed Here.

THERE, NO LONGER

I went back to Kuala Lumpur to attend the Asia 21 Young Leaders Summit in 2009. My parents came with me. We tried to find the house we used to live in, but the city had changed beyond all recognition. They couldn't quite remember the exact address, and now there were too many new highways and high-rise shopping malls for my father to 'feel' his way back to a place he could once drive to without even thinking about it.

We gave up and went to Petaling Street, Chinatown, for a plate of KL Hokkien mee at Kim Lian Kee. The narrow staircase leading upstairs was poky, there were granite-topped, dark wood tables and stools, and the toilet floor was disgustingly wet. For a moment we were ecstatic because it all looked and smelled so familiar that it felt like a homecoming. Then the crunch of deep-fried pork lard in that first mouthful of Hokkien noodles coated with dark soy sauce! 'This is quite authentic,' my father said – there is no higher praise. Later, though, they tried to find the places they used to go to, and the other foods they used to eat. Nothing else was the same. Everyone they knew had moved away, all the shops they used to frequent had shut down. We were nothing but tourists in this city.

I suppose the trouble for all migrants who come *here* and go back *there* is that when you get there, as Gertrude Stein famously said, there isn't any *there* there. We got back onto the plane and flew over the sea to sky, to come back here.

SAMINA YASMEEN

Tape and Memory

I recently discovered a cassette tape my mother and brother recorded and sent to me a month after I arrived in Canberra as a student in 1979. Mixed in with many others, I could have mistaken this relic to be an old recording of the legendary Indian female singer Lata Mangeshkar, or the equally gifted Pakistani Ghazal singer Mehdi Hassan, but the date on it suddenly made me realise its significance.

'It carries my mumma's voice,' I thought to myself.

Having lost my dear mother in 2003, I had longed to hear her voice, see her face, and share all those stories that we shared wherever we happened to be. Knowing that the tape would once again enable me to hear her melodious voice, singing laughter and cheeky remarks should have made it easier for me to listen to it. 'But will I be able to deal with it?' I asked myself.

And so I left it sitting in the drawer until a warm afternoon when I sat in my car – the only place where I could play an old cassette – parked in the driveway with a pine tree providing the shade and privacy that I needed, tears rolling down my cheeks.

My mother had had my youngest brother, Nadeem Iqbal, with her as she made the recording; he was studying medicine in Rawalpindi. Together they provided me a glimpse of the world I had recently left, to study International Relations at the Australian National University. She talked of all the friends who had visited home. She called relatives and asked them to record messages for me on the tape, laughed in between them and scolded my brother frequently. I found out that she had not lost the last two kilos she wanted to lose, then heard my brother advising her irreverently that the cheese she was devouring would not help. She complained and laughed at the same time.

I remembered all those moments when she would react to similar comments from my brothers, knowing that I would put my arms around her and say, 'Just ignore these useless sons of yours, Mumma.' They would retort, 'Ammi, don't listen to this daughter. She always leads you astray.' My brother did not spare me either, 'Hey Meena! What is this, asking for a first-aid kit from Pakistan? The air marshal who is carrying this tape for you all the way to Australia cannot be expected to cart a first-aid kit as well. Don't tell me that there is no pharmacy in Canberra.'

I laughed amidst my tears. It was silly of me to expect an air marshal to carry bandage, iodine and aspirin on his first official visit to Australia. But as a new student in 1979, how was I to know the ease with which I could buy these things only half a kilometre away from ANU?

Hearing Mum's voice, Nadeem's reportage of my other two siblings, Ghalib and Ghazala, and Dad's short sentences made me laugh. I remembered the sense of dislocation I'd felt all those years ago when I heard this tape for the first time, and I realised a little more about the woman I have grown up to be.

Listening to the tape under the shade of a pine tree, with some of its branches touching the fence and others conversing with the towering eucalyptus tree, sitting in my car, parked in the driveway outside the home I share with my husband, James – I realised anew that I have a home in Australia. I am *at home* in Australia. And this has all happened not through some carefully devised plan... it just happened.

There was once a day I looked back and realised that ten years had passed without my feeling 'away from home'. Today, as I write, I realise that thirty-three years have gone by, matching the number of our home on the wooden letterbox, hung by James on the pine tree beside my car.

My soul is not burdened by the loss of these years. I feel light, and sense the sun smiling beyond the shade of the pine tree. When I listen to that cassette, the moment tells me that as the melodious sound of my mother's voice enters the deep recesses of my soul and takes me home, finding this cassette would have been traumatically painful had I not visited Pakistan regularly, curled up to my mother, laughed with her, annoyed her, read Gibran with her, or spent nights just talking with her. I also know how the passing moments could have scarred my soul if I had felt alienated in this new environment. But I did not.

Instead, completing my PhD, working in the state parliament and then teaching at the University of Western Australia bound me to this country in ways I could not comprehend when that tape first arrived.

My students are my friends. They have shared a path to knowledge with me. They have taught me about music, the latest software and Australian fads. Sometimes I feel frustrated at my inability to keep up with the latest fashions and ideas. A student once banged his head on the table when I referred to Pink Floyd as 'the latest music'. I recall another nearly hiding under the table, hoping that I would not embarrass him with naughty comments about good-looking men in front of his superiors.

I have my adopted Serbian children – they may not be mine legally or biologically, but their affection soothes my heart. I am also the adopted daughter of a true-blue Aussie mother – again, not legally, but that doesn't matter to any of us. Ethnicity, religion, migration experiences and history lose their loaded meaning. We are bound by love – of ideas, feelings and belonging.

Listening to that cassette, I remembered the young woman I was, newly arrived in Australia, both sure and unsure of the place I was to be based in for the next year. My father studied architecture at the University of Melbourne when we were young; we remained in Pakistan with our mother. All of the postcards and photographs that he sent, with lengthy commentaries in his neat handwriting, taught us what they could about Australia and its people. He'd sent innumerable photographs of buildings and their designs. Exploring Canberra, I felt as if I had been to this city before.

Walking through the maze of the Coombs building, with its connected hexagonal sections, I was pleased to recognise names adorning the offices of the professors whose publications I had read as a student at Quaid-e-Azam University, Islamabad. So this is where my mother so lovingly sent me to study, I would think, then miss her achingly. I thought of the poetry, art, laughter and ideas I had left behind. I missed the security of being with my family, being taken care of and being spoilt rotten. This is why I felt it appropriate that Mum send me a first-aid kit.

But there was another reason I longed for the spoils of home: I had little idea of how to deal with money. I had been instructed by Nadeem to send him a pair of jeans through the returning air marshal; I vividly remember walking through the Canberra shopping arcade with a newly made friend, Leigh, in pursuit of some.

On my first excursion involving transactions – in Australian dollars, no less – I asked Leigh, 'Do you think

I have sufficient money to buy a new pair of jeans?'

'How much money do you have?' he asked.

'Two hundred dollars.'

'I am not walking with you just in case you're mugged,' he replied.

It took me years to work out that one does not need such large sums to buy Levi's' jeans.

The years here have moved faster than I anticipated, but they have taught me to appreciate beauty in more ways than the ones I learnt through my mother. She adored flowers: jasmine and jonquils adorned our home garden in Pakistan. She would smell them slowly in early mornings, weave them into her hair – an act that earned her the name Aunty Motia (Jasmine) – and leave them sitting at the table. I love these flowers the way my mother did.

Every autumn, James plants jonquil bulbs in our garden, so that Mum's love for them survives at our home, thousands of miles away from hers. Seasonally, the jasmine bush that grows by the retreat in our home reminds me of my mother, just as that cassette recording does from time to time. The jasmine's perfume carries with it memories of my mother – and with it, her joy, her Pakistan – though the scent here in Australia is never of the same intensity as it was there.

Western Australia has opened my eyes to another kind of beauty – its wildflowers. Friends introduced me to these flowers when I arrived in Perth in 1988, but it was James who showed me their intricate patterns. Wandering through our farm near Wandering, WA (that really is the town's name), he takes pictures of these flowers that make me speechless at the beauty God has created. I find myself asking friends and family to visit Perth during spring, and I wish my mother were here to walk with me. She would have cheekily remarked, 'Our flowers are better than yours' – while gathering some to take home.

♠

The cassette stops. I have learnt to appreciate silence. In Islamabad, I grew up in a home frequented by writers, artists, politicians – the rich and famous, the poor and destitute. Mum's love for Urdu literature and those who created it meant all those passing through the city had a room available in our home. The writer Mumtaz Mufti once likened our home to a busy crossing, and pondered how the children could study. But my mother always found time that was just hers. She would sit by the fire at night, reading books, and just *be*.

As I look at today's Pakistan, Urdu literature is losing its appeal among younger generations. Reading traditional books has been consigned to the annals of history, and the love of Urdu poetry, that nuanced and multi-layered expression of beauty, seems to have been lost in the Pakistan of today. Technology rules with bite-sized snippets of what one hears from a friend about literature, and the real stories get lost. I read a commentary on a poem by Ibn-e-Insha, a famous Pakistani poet, that he wrote after he was diagnosed with Hodgkin's disease: the series of 'authoritative comments' totally miss the point that it was written for my mother, who had offered to donate a few years of her life to him. It is not much different from the re-creation of realities through iPhones, tablets and Google in our new world – the age I have entered as an Australian – but I do wonder if that commentary's tone also results from the incessant noise in the Pakistan of today.

Noise pollution rules Pakistan in all forms, be it politics, culture or the roadside. Searching for silence can be a disheartening process. Locals wonder why would you do it, anyway? James and I recently spent ten glorious days in Gwadar – sitting on a veranda, looking over the city from the comfort of the Pearl Continental hotel, and reading books. Once the intelligence agency discovered our presence in this port city, one at the centre of a regional strategic struggle where the presence of foreigners is closely monitored, they found it unfathomable that we had travelled all the way from Perth to the beaches of Gwadar to read books and enjoy silence. As an Australian, I need space, silence and serenity when I want it.

And it is amidst the silence, at our farm, standing on weathered granite outcrops as old as the earth, that I once again hear my mother's voice the way I did when I discovered that cassette. She is telling me jokes and stories, and laughing. Her lyrical giggles touch the space in my soul that is my essence, my identity. Today I am far more than the young Pakistani woman who arrived as a student in Australia all those years ago in 1979. I am an Australian who has subconsciously acquired habits, ideas and belief systems unknown to me when the cassette arrived.

My identity shifts constantly in the eyes of other Australians. Sometimes I am simply treated as a 'stock' Australian who has the rights and responsibilities shared by all other citizens. Then there are times when I am an Australian woman who also happens to be a Muslim. On 9/11, as the towers collapsed and the dust rose above the New York streets, my Muslim identity took on a new meaning. An unfamiliar and threatening darkness rolled overhead. Friends and colleagues saw it coming: they sent me messages of support against a possible backlash springing from searing grief experienced in those days. Others – strangers – sent me emails of hatred, wishing me death. It was as if they only wanted to hear the eerie sounds that come from playing that cassette tape backwards: they refused to hear the same melody and love that they feel for Australia as I do.

I wondered then as I wonder now – as we all remembered 9/11 and the Bali bombings – if those who wished me death as a Muslim could know the shock my family experienced.

They would never know of the stillness in my brother Ghalib's voice as he felt the heavy crush of international pressure as a member of Pakistan's Foreign Service.

They would never appreciate my sister Ghazala's courage, setting off, as she usually did, to work at the hospital on that carefree sunny morning. As she arrived, she faced the sudden fierce fury of national media in her capacity as the first ever female chairperson of the Greater St Louis Muslim Association. She stared at the cameras as she firmly and calmly voiced the American Muslim hurt and outrage at the tragic events.

They would never know of the tears my mother shed on that night, and again as the attacks on Afghanistan and Iraq began. They will never hear the stories of innocent Pakistanis sliced by suicide bombings, or suffering the trauma of seeing others die beside them: the shock of survival. As for cassettes, no matter whose, they will only ever play it backwards.

AUTHOR BIOGRAPHIES

SHALINI AKHIL's first novel, *The Bollywood Beauty*, was published in 2005. She has been short-listed in the Victorian Premier's Literary Awards and made it through to a Raw Comedy National Grand Final. Her work has been published in various anthologies. Born in Fiji, Akhil currently lives with her husband in Melbourne and is working on her second novel.

ALI ALIZADEH's books include the collection of poetry *Ashes in the Air*, the creative family history *Iran: My Grandfather* and the novel *The New Angel*. His next novel will be published by University of Queensland Press in 2013. He was born in Iran and migrated to Australia at fourteen. Alizadeh holds a PhD in Professional Writing from Deakin University and is a lecturer in Creative Writing at Monash University. He lives with his wife and son in Melbourne.

DIANE ARMSTRONG is a freelance journalist with over 3000 articles published in Australian and international publications. Her awards include the Pluma de Plata from the Government of Mexico and the George Munster Award for Independent Journalism. Armstrong's *Mosaic: A Chronicle of Five Generations* was short-listed for the Victorian Premier's Literary Award for Non-Fiction and for the National Biography Award. *The Voyage of Their Life: The Story of the SS Derna and its Passengers* was short-listed for the NSW Premier's Literary Awards. *Winter Journey* has been translated into Polish and Hebrew and was short-listed for the Commonwealth Writers' Prize.

DEBORAH CARLYON was born in Goroka, Papua New Guinea, from the heart of a proud Chimbu heritage. She studied Steiner Education and became the founding teacher for the Noosa Pengari Steiner School in 1996. Carlyon won the 2001 Queensland Premier's Literary Award – Best Emerging Author for *Mama Kuma: One Woman, Two Cultures*, for which she also received a Centenary Medal Award for contribution to society through literature. Her *Loku and the Shark Attack* was shortlisted for the 2007 Patricia Wrightson Prize.

VAL COLIC-PEISKER is an associate professor in sociology at RMIT. She has worked as a journalist, author, translator and radio producer in Zagreb, Croatia. Colic-Peisker has published extensively in mainstream and academic media. She has published widely, including *Split Lives: Croatian Australian Stories* and *Migration, Class and Transnational Identities: Croatians in Australia and America*. Since 2009, she has been the convenor of the interuniversity Migration and Mobility Research Network, based at RMIT.

MARK DAPIN moved to Australia in the late 1980s from the UK. He is the author of *Strange Country* and *King of the Cross*, and has been editor-in-chief of ACP's men's magazines. He lives in Sydney with his partner and two children.

AMY ESPESETH is a writer, publisher and academic. She is the recipient of the Felix Meyer Scholarship in Literature, the Victorian Premier's Literary Award for an Unpublished Manuscript, the QUT Postgraduate Creative Writing Prize and the CAL/Scribe Fiction Prize. As the publisher at Vignette Press, Espeseth continues their acclaimed subcultural 'mook' series. Her first novel, *Sufficient Grace*, was published in 2012 and her second, *Trouble Telling the Weather*, will be published in 2013.

LILY YULIANTI FARID was born and raised in Makassar, Indonesia. She worked as a reporter of the *Kompas* daily from 1996 until 2000. In 2010, she began a PhD in Gender and Media from the University of Melbourne. She worked as a radio program specialist/producer of *Radio Japan NHK*, Tokyo. During this period, she also worked as a columnist for *Nytid News Magazine* in Norway. Her second short-story collection, *Family Room*, was translated into English and selected for the Modern Library of Indonesia series. Farid is director of the Makassar International Writers Festival.

CHRIS FLYNN is the books editor at *The Big Issue* and author of the novel *A Tiger in Eden*. He has written for the *Griffith Review*, *Meanjin*, *The Paris Review*, *Monster Children*, *McSweeney's* and many other publications.

JUAN GARRIDO-SALGADO was born in Chile and was a political prisoner under the Pinochet regime. His books have been published in Chile, Colombia, Spain, El Salvador, Brazil, Europe, New Zealand and Australia. He is also an accomplished translator, specifically of Aboriginal works into Spanish.

ROANNA GONSALVES is an Indian–Australian writer who was born and brought up in Mumbai, India. Her work includes a play, *Yet to Ascertain the Nature of the Crime*, that won an Australian Writers Guild Award, an illustrated essay/radio documentary for ABC Radio National's *360documentaries* program, and numerous short stories. Gonsalves is undertaking a PhD at the University of NSW, where she is conducting an empirical study of the globalised literary field.

GHASSAN HAGE is the Future Generation Professor of Anthropology and Social Theory at the University of Melbourne. He has written extensively in the comparative anthropology of nationalism, racism and multiculturalism. His most well-known works are *White Nation: Fantasies of White Supremacy in a Multicultural Society* and *Against Paranoid Nationalism: Searching for Hope in a Shrinking Society*.

DMETRI KAKMI's fictionalised memoir, *Mother Land*, was short-listed for the NSW Premier's Literary Awards. His essays, journalism and short stories have appeared in various newspaper and magazines, and he is the editor of the children's anthologies *When We Were Young* and the forthcoming *13 Ghosts*. His body lives in Melbourne and his heart in Istanbul.

DANNY KATZ, Canadian-born, came to Australia at a young age. After failed careers as a musician, stand-up comedian and car washer, he finally turned to writing and became a newspaper columnist for the *Age*, the *Sydney Morning Herald* and the *Western Australian*. He is also the author of the books *S.C.U.M.*, *Spit the Dummy*, *Dork Geek Jew* and the *Little Lunch* series for children.

ADIB KHAN came to Australia to study English Literature at Monash University. Khan's first novel, *Seasonal Adjustments*, won the Christina Stead Prize for Fiction and the Book of the Year in the NSW Premier's Literature Awards in 1994. His second novel, *Solitude of Illusions*, was short-listed for the Christina Stead Prize for Fiction and the Ethnic Commission Award in the NSW Premier's Literature Awards in 1997.

MEG MUNDELL was born and raised in Aotearoa/New Zealand, and now lives in Melbourne. She spent five years at *The Big Issue*. Her first novel, *Black Glass*, was Highly Commended in the 2012 Barbara Jefferis Award, and short-listed for the 2010 CAL/Scribe Fiction Prize, the 2011 Aurealis Awards, and the 2012 Norma K Hemming Award.

MALLA NUNN was born in Swaziland, Southern Africa, and currently lives in Sydney, Australia. She is a filmmaker with three award-winning films to her credit and is at work on her next crime novel.

ALICE PUNG is the author of *Her Father's Daughter* and *Unpolished Gem* and the editor of *Growing up Asian in Australia*. *Unpolished Gem* won the 2007 Australian Newcomer of the Year award in the Australian Book Industry Awards, and was short-listed for the Victorian Premier's Literary Awards, the NSW Premier's Literary Awards and the *Age* Book of the Year Award 2007.

CATHERINE REY's first novel, *L'Ami Intime (The Intimate Friend)*, was published in 1994, followed by *Les Jours Heureux* and *Eloge de l'Oubli (Praise of Forgetfulness)*. Since then, Rey has published the books *Lucie Comme les Chiens*, *Ce que Racontait* and *Les Extraordinaires Aventures de John Lofty Oakes* in English, with the titles of *The Spruiker's Tale* and *Stepping Out* respectively. Rey currently teaches at the University of Western Sydney.

MICHAEL SALA was born in Holland and grew up moving between Europe and Australia. His novel, *The Last Thread*, was published in 2012. He lives in Newcastle with his wife and children and works as a teacher at high school and the University of Newcastle.

HSU-MING TEO is a novelist and cultural historian based at Macquarie University, Sydney. Her first novel, *Love and Vertigo*, won the *Australian/Vogel* Literary Award, and her second novel, *Behind the Moon*, was short-listed for the NSW Premier's Literary Awards. Her academic publications include *Cultural History in Australia* and *Desert Passions: Orientalism and Romance Novels*.

MICHELLE AUNG THIN was born in Burma during the year of a military coup d'état. Thin's first novel, *The Monsoon Bride*, was short-listed for the Victorian Premier's Literary Award for an Unpublished Manuscript in 2010 and won a Readings Foundation/Wheeler Centre Fellowship. Michelle is the recipient of a Canada Council for the Arts grant. Thin is completing a PhD in Creative Writing at the University of Adelaide. She lives with her family in Melbourne.

PAOLA TOTARO is a prominent Australian journalist and writer now based in London. She is a former Europe correspondent for the *Sydney Morning Herald* and the *Age*. She is vice president of the Foreign Press Association in London and writes for the *Guardian*, the *Independent* and *New Statesman*. She has degrees in politics and Italian, and contributes regularly to the BBC.

MARIA TUMARKIN is the author of *Traumascapes* and *Courage*. Her latest book, *Otherland*, was short-listed for the Victorian and NSW Premier's Literary Awards and the *Age* Book of the Year. She frequently collaborates with visual artists, musicians and other writers. She holds a PhD in Cultural History from the University of Melbourne. Between 2008 and 2010, Tumarkin was a Research Fellow on an international, ARC-funded 'Social Memory and Historical Justice' project.

CHI VU was born in Vietnam and came to Australia in 1979. Vu's plays include the critically acclaimed and widely studied *Vietnam: A Psychic Guide*; her short stories have appeared in various publications, including the *Macquarie PEN Anthology of Australian Literature* and *Growing Up Asian in Australia*. Vu's gothic novella, *Anguli Ma*, was recently published.

ALEXIS WRIGHT is a member of the Waanyi Nation of the southern highlands of the Gulf of Carpentaria. Her writings include the novels *Plains of Promise*, *Carpentaria*, *The Swan Book* and the non-fiction book *Grog War*, and she was the compiler and editor of *Take Power*. She is a Distinguished Research Fellow in the Writing and Society Research Group, University of Western Sydney.

SAMINA YASMEEN is director of the Centre for Muslim States and Societies and lectures in Political Science and International Relations in the School of Social and Cultural Studies at the University of Western Australia. She is the author of *Understanding Muslim Identities: From Perceived Relative Exclusion to Inclusion*.

OUYANG YU came to Australia in early 1991. He edits Australia's only Chinese literary journal, *Otherland*. His books include *The Eastern Slope Chronicle* and *The English Class*; collections of poetry, *Songs of the Last Chinese Poet* and *New and Selected Poems*; and translations in Chinese, *The Female Eunuch*, *The Ancestor Game*. *The English Class* was named one of the best books of 2010 in *Australian Book Review*, the *Age* and the *Sydney Morning Herald*. It won the Community Relations Award in the 2011 NSW Premier's Literary Awards.

ARNOLD ZABLE is an acclaimed writer, novelist and human rights advocate, and president of the Melbourne centre of PEN International. His books include *Jewels and Ashes*, *The Fig Tree*, *Violin Lessons* and three novels: *Café Scheherazade*, *Scraps of Heaven* and *Sea of Many Returns*. Zable has conducted writing workshops throughout Australia, working with refugees, immigrants, the homeless, the deaf and Black Saturday bushfire survivors. He has a doctorate in Creative Arts from the University of Melbourne, where he was recently appointed a Vice Chancellor's Fellow.

ACKNOWLEDGEMENTS

from KENT MacCARTER

I would like to thank Martin Hughes, Rebecca Starford, Ali Lemer, Belle Place, Arnold Zable, Alexis Wright, JM Coetzee, Andrew Riemer, Mungo MacCallum and all of the contributors for their belief in, support for and commitment to this collection.

Special thanks go to my wife, Penelope Goodes, for her endless tips and help. I would also like to thank Erica Sontheimer, Martin Shaw, Ivor Indyk, Mirka Mora, Josi Smith, Jacqueline Dutton, David Carlin, Alison Barker, Renee Senogles, Jane Novak and the Melbourne PEN executive committee for the help, support and promotion of this collection as it was being researched, written and edited.

A big thanks is also due to my fellow members of 'Men's Group' – Julian Novitz, Aaron Mannion, Amy Espeseth and Emmett Stinson – who continue to help me refine what it takes to tell a story by writing and editing one.

from ALI LEMER

Many thanks to Martin Hughes and Rebecca Starford at Affirm Press for their unalloyed support, and to Arnold Zable, Alexis Wright, JM Coetzee and all of the authors who contributed their writing to the book; especially copious thanks are due to my co-editor, Kent MacCarter, for his tireless efforts on behalf of this project. I'm also grateful to Mark Batt, Amy Espeseth, Jenny Lee and Melanie Dankel for their personal support and encouragement.